W9-DEX-555

THE NATIONAL LANGUAGE QUESTION

THE NATIONAL LANGUAGE QUESTION

Linguistic Problems of Newly Independent States

R. B. Le PAGE

Published for the
Institute of Race Relations, London

OXFORD UNIVERSITY PRESS
LONDON NEW YORK

Oxford University Press, Ely House, London W. 1

GLASGOW NEW YORK TORONTO MELBOURNE WELLINGTON
CAPE TOWN SALISBURY IBADAN NAIROBI DAR ES SALAAM LUSAKA ADDIS ABABA
BOMBAY CALCUTTA MADRAS KARACHI LAHORE DACCA
KUALA LUMPUR SINGAPORE HONG KONG TOKYO

ISBN 0 19 218147 5

First published 1964
Reprinted 1966 and 1971

Set in Great Britain by R. J. Acford Ltd. Chichester
and reprinted lithographically by
Headley Brothers Ltd, Ashford Kent

CONTENTS

PREFACE

I should like to acknowledge the free use I have made of papers and reports presented by my colleagues at the CCTA/CSA Symposium on Multilingualism held at Brazzaville in July 1962—papers which unfortunately have not yet been printed. I attended this Symposium as a result of the generosity of the Ford Foundation. I am indebted to the Commonwealth High Commissions and Foreign Embassies in Kuala Lumpur for the help given in collecting data about their countries, and to friends in Sarawak and Sabah who were both hospitable and helpful to me on field trips. My colleagues and students in the University of Malaya have contributed a great deal to the following pages and I am grateful to them for their kindness and patience. Finally I must confess that, since my own direct experience of the problems discussed is limited to fourteen years' teaching and research in the West Indies and South-East Asia, I have when dealing with other countries plagiarised freely the publications listed in the short bibliography at the end of this book.

R. B. LE PAGE.

University of Malaya

1 *January*, 1964.

INTRODUCTION

SINCE the end of the Second World War a great many new nation-states have emerged from the former colonial empires to claim their seats, one by one, at the United Nations. Most of them share a number of common problems, political, economic and cultural. What form of government will prove stable and well-suited to the new country? How can the economy best be developed to the point where its self-sustaining growth will enable the new state to feed its rapidly increasing population and give them a standard of living comparable to that which they see older states enjoying? Many people would feel that these—the political and economic questions—are the basic questions. And yet in many ways, as I shall try to show in this book, the cultural questions are the most fundamental. The reason is that so many of these new states owe their frontiers to the old colonial régimes which, for motives of their own—administrative convenience, or the geography of white exploration and settlement—gave a sometimes spurious unity to regions which had little otherwise to recommend them as national entities. One of the first problems therefore which the states have to resolve is whether they exist as anything more than artificial political entities. Very often cultural unity must be imposed, a sense of belonging to a nation must be induced in disparate sections of the population, before the processes of government or economic progress can be given any direction.

The acquisition of language was, biologically, the basic requirement for man's survival as a species. Students of language today are behavioural scientists, and linguistics is the key without which none of the behavioural sciences can be satisfactorily unlocked; it is a discipline almost as basic to the behavioural sciences as mathematics is to the physical sciences. Until quite recently linguistics—the scientific study of language—had been primarily concerned with the internal structures of language; but in recent years linguists have been forced to take more and more account of the structuring of environment that linguistic habits represent; they have been forced to collaborate more and more closely with the anthropologist, the psychologist and the sociologist in order to try to solve the problems with which they have all been confronted.

One reason for this is as follows: the linguist, by studying the internal structure of a language, can describe that language so that the foreigner can learn it; further, by comparing the structure of the language to be learned with that of the native language of the learner the linguist can predict what difficulties the learner is likely to have. Linguists therefore have been able for a number of years to give helpful advice on the teaching of languages, and that advice has been sought by a number of the newly-emergent nations which needed to impose a common language in which to conduct their business. But the linguist arriving in such a situation found to his dismay that the whole question of what language to speak and what languages to teach was bedevilled from the outset by a whole host of factors over which he had no control and of which in the past he had had very little experience, which proved nevertheless to be extremely relevant to the language problem. These problems belong to the fields of politics, anthropology, psychology and social psychology.

It is generally recognised that the language problems facing the new nations are not themselves new by any means; parallels can be found from all periods of history and all parts of the world. What is new, however, is the extreme urgency of solving the economic and political problems of the world, because of the population explosion on the one hand and of the threat of nuclear explosions on the other. Language barriers are certainly barriers to economic progress, as any one who has had experience of rural development work in underdeveloped countries will agree. Are language barriers also barriers to international understanding? Some maintain that if everybody in the world spoke the same language, there would be no international disagreements. This is a more doubtful thesis. It is undoubtedly true that language is the key to education; but it is also true, unfortunately, that education can increase faction in a community sometimes, rather than reduce it.

In this short book I have attempted to outline an objective approach to the problem, illustrating each factor by reference to the actual situation in various parts of the world. Two case-histories are presented in some detail: that of India, a country of many languages but with a long cultural history unifying the speakers of those languages, and that of Malaysia, a country whose diverse language-groups have little common cultural history except that provided by a comparatively short period of British colonial rule. No attempt has been made to prescribe an answer to the problems; the book is directed at an understanding of the factors involved.

I. THE FUNCTION OF LANGUAGE FOR THE INDIVIDUAL

In the long evolutionary history of the organic world, each species that has survived has done so by reason of its inherited capacity to come to terms with its environment. Man is no exception to this rule. The human species is in some ways rather badly equipped for survival, being not particularly well-protected against extremes of heat and cold, of humidity or dryness, not particularly strong in comparison with some animals, not particularly swift in comparison with others. In particular, the human infant is many years coming to maturity, and needs the protection and succour of the social organisation—whether it is the basic unit of that organisation, the family, or some other unit—if it is to survive to maturity.

Man has, however, one enormous advantage over other species in that, genetically, he inherits the capacity for language. This capacity resides in his intelligence on the one hand and his capacity for certain muscular responses on the other. Given the intelligence, any set of muscular responses could be conditioned, coded and learnt as a language. The fact that we make most use initially of those muscular responses which produce noise, rather than those which are only visible, for linguistic purposes, is probably due simply to the fact that speech can be heard around corners and in the dark, whereas other muscular responses would have to be seen or felt to be understood. Written language is a secondary development; it, again, is a system of coding responses. The system in this case is usually—but not always—closely related to that of the spoken language, and its particular advantage is that of permanence.

The human species has survived because of its capacity for inventiveness, which has enabled it to deal with changes in its environment which might otherwise have been disastrous, and its capacity for social organisation, which has enabled it to put up a collective defence against its enemies and to make collective provision against emergency. Both of these capacities depend upon language. Inventiveness, however, is a characteristic of the individual, and is often at odds with the demands of the social organisation. We shall see later why this is.

In order to be inventive language itself is not necessary, but some process of conceptual analysis of one's environment similar to that which forms the mental basis for language is necessary, and without language cannot proceed very far. In order to transmit the results of one's creative thinking to society, language is certainly necessary, just as it is necessary in order that one generation may transmit its knowledge to the next. Let us look first therefore at the processes of conceptual analysis.

When a baby is born it responds instinctively to its environment in order to survive, but the categories into which that environment is divided are probably very simple and few in number: different shades of light and darkness, discomfort as contrasted with a sense of well-being, freedom of movement or lack of freedom—beyond these and perhaps a few more categories the world for the baby is undifferentiated. From the moment that he is born however, he starts to learn through the conditioning of his reflex actions. Both the baby and his parents become conditioned to one another, learn to recognise the sounds and movements made by one another, memorise these in the contexts in which they occur, recall and repeat those sounds or movements if they wish to recreate the context, and in this way, through the process known as instrumental learning—a particular kind of conditioning of the reflexes—the baby learns the language of its parents and learns to differentiate its environment by means of those categories which its parents use. There is a certain amount of evidence that children without access to language for one reason or another—perhaps because they are born blind and deaf—

nevertheless develop through their other senses an analysis of their world into categories which are sufficiently sophisticated for them to carry out the process which we know as thinking. They will learn to divide their world up into hard objects and soft objects, hot and cold, wet and dry, memorising and to a certain extent analysing their sensations; but without help, and without the process of conceptual analysis through the use of some kind of language, their thinking will remain at a rudimentary level.

The baby instinctively explores the use of all his muscles and limbs and organs. His instinct to vocalise is reinforced by the fact that his crying brings comfort and his babbling, which is a form of exploration of his powers undertaken when his physical needs have been satisfied, brings a warm and loving response from those around him. His babbled noises are very often echoed by his parents, and he re-echoes them. This pattern of babbled response, echo and re-echo, is reinforced in the conditioning process by the general atmosphere of love and attention which it generates, by the tickling and the dandling that accompanies it; it thus forms a strongly-desired pattern for the imitation of actual linguistic responses which follows.

The child may first become aware of the sound of the word *dog* as part of a number of contexts which to begin with may have a great many things in common—the same garden, perhaps, the same voices around and so on—the shaggy bounding animal being only one part of the general scene in which this word *dog* recurs in such phrases as *good dog, bad dog*; however, the fact that these phrases are uttered at moments when the shaggy animal is particularly prominent on the scene will help to associate them more closely with the animal, and quite quickly the process of discrimination will be reinforced by *dog* indoors, *dog* on walks, 'let the dog out, John', until the sight of a shaggy animal is sufficient to recall the sound of the word *dog* to the child more powerfully than any of the other sounds it has heard, and it will be stimulated to try to utter this sound as its own response. If the attempt is successful the conditioning of the child's response may be further reinforced by the pleasure shown by its parents and perhaps by their echoing the response. If on some subsequent occasion the child sees a goat and responds with the word *dog*, that response will not be reinforced by the parents and the process of discrimination will be carried one stage farther. The type of shaggy animal which the sound of the word *dog* will recall will become progressively limited, and in this way, which I have illustrated very crudely, the child acquires the same categories for analysing its perception of its environment as its parents.

The child acquires something else also—an understanding of the process of discrimination itself. As we grow up we tend to extrapolate this process of discrimination as far as we can, in order to abstract from our experience a set of concepts which seem to us to represent the quintessential characteristics of the categories which we have learned. Such mental concepts can, as I said earlier, be formed without the use of language, but the process of language-learning and the acquisition of categorised linguistic responses help us to bring our mental concepts much more sharply into focus and to label them for purposes of recall by means of the easily-remembered labels for categories which make up the morphemes of our language.

As we become endowed with concepts in this manner, we explore the use of our mental powers by recombining them in patterns and combinations in a creative way, the new combinations provoking linguistic responses different from any that we have heard, but created to a large extent by analogy with patterns with which we are already familiar. These patterns are the grammar of our language, which we have learned from our parents just as we have learned the vocabulary.

Not only, then, do our parents and those around us condition us as we grow up to see the world through their eyes, to analyse our perception of our environment according to their own categories, and so by the process of extrapolation to form concepts which are to a very large extent similar to their concepts, but they also provide us with the grammatical patterns which to a very large extent condition the ways in which we can recombine our concepts—in other words, the ways in which we can think creatively.

It is important to remember that the 'meaning' of a linguistic response (an utterance that is) is that it is a response to a certain context or situation. Also, that concepts are formed by extrapolating the process of discrimination as one context after another comes to be identified with the same utterance. The 'meaning' therefore of the words with which we express our concept, and the concept itself, must always remain personal to each one of us to the extent that they derive whatever reality they have from our own personal experience. We may share our experience with others; language only works as a means of communication to the extent that the experiences, including the linguistic experiences, of a group of people overlap. We may regard the common factors in our experiences as representing the dictionary meanings of the words we use, but these words have no meanings as long as they remain inside the dictionary—they only acquire meaning by being uttered, and the meaning they acquire is that they are the response we make to our environment at any particular moment. No concepts therefore can be finally detached from or abstracted from the person who conceived them, nor from the circumstances under which he conceived them. For the student of linguistics, treated as a behavioural science, the idea of *universals*, concepts which have some universal significance quite independent of the person who conceived them or the circumstances from which they derive, is a chimera of certain schools of philosophy. Were it possible to envisage concepts having an independent existence of their own it would be possible to conceive of a universal language through which those concepts could be manipulated, a language independent of any language community, and unchanging throughout the ages. The language of symbolic logic and the language of mathematics are the nearest we are likely to get to such a universal language, and neither of these is truly independent of historical circumstances. Artificial languages such as Esperanto are neither universal in their patterns of conceptual analysis, nor organic. They are thus no answer to the problems that confront us in this book.

We can now see the nature of the essential functions that language performs for the individual. As an individual grows up in or lives in a speech-community, the acquisition of the speech-habits of that community allows him to become a full member of the society, contributing his responses to the common stock in such a manner that they will be easily recognised and stimulate responses from others which he in turn can understand. He can thus identify himself with and become part of a larger unit, making his contribution to its resources and drawing upon its resources. The need for acts of communion with others is basic to man, part of his gregarious instinct; most of us crave for speech with our fellow men in the same way that we crave for love. Language is not primarily a means of communication but a means of communion; to say 'Good morning' to an acquaintance in the street and to receive his response is analogous to shaking hands or holding hands. To be alone in a strange city where nobody can be made to understand one's language can be a frightening experience.

Perfect communion would require complete identity of response, and can perhaps only be even approximately achieved by identical twins. For most of us, communion with other people is very imperfect indeed, but at the level of daily intercourse we will get the greatest sense of relaxation when we are among those whose linguistic responses are closest to our own. Being among strangers is often stimulating, but one can rarely be completely relaxed because one is uncertain how to respond and uncertain how one's own responses will be interpreted. To return to one's native city after a spell abroad and hear familiar accents, see familiar gestures and mannerisms, can be like putting on a comfortable old suit of clothes after having been slightly uncomfortable in a new suit. One is often not aware of the slight strain while one is away, but the sense of relief on one's return is noticeable. If on the other hand one was disgusted with one's own city when one left, then one may still react with disgust to the sound of one's native language when one returns.

The next important function that language fulfils for the individual is that it allows him greater possibilities of self-expression that he would have without it. Here we must pause for a moment to consider what it is we mean by 'self-expression'. The behavioural scientist analyses all behaviour in terms of stimulus and response. The stimulus comes to us from our environment, from the behaviour of others around us, from our own consciously- or unconsciously-remembered past; our response at each moment of our lives, if it is a total response, will be a release of energy equal to the resultant of all the forces operating on us at that moment, and the form it takes will be determined by our inherited and acquired characteristics and by the situation in which we find ourselves. The use of the vocal organs for making noises is simply one set of co-ordinated muscular responses, similar to the use of the legs for running away from danger or of the arms for fighting off danger. But running away and fighting and shouting are crude responses to crudely-apprehended stimuli. Such reactions do not often provide a completely adequate response to the infinitely more subtle stimuli operating on the heightened sensibility and self-awareness of intelligent man. He is aware, sometimes faintly, sometimes very sharply, not only of the stimuli operating on him but of certain patterns of recurrence in those stimuli, and by a process of extrapolation similar to that which, as we saw earlier, leads to the formation of concepts, he is driven to try to find and express the over-all intricate pattern of his own existence. He may find his most satisfactory release of tension through dancing, or through working with his hands, or through speech or writing or painting, but whatever the mode of expression, it must be articulate—that is, a succession of muscular responses joined to one another so as to express his search for pattern and order. In speech he will adopt to begin with the phonemic, morphemic, syntactic and semantic patterns of the speech community with which he feels most closely identified, since these are the patterns which have evolved over the centuries as a means of response by that community to its environment; but, since every individual is unique, each must sooner or later create his own idiom if he is to achieve a completely satisfying release of his own tension. Every artist therefore is a lonely individual creating his own idiom, but as we saw earlier, he is also a member of society needing a response from society, and since his idiom is strange that response is unlikely to be one which will give him a sense of complete identity with the society in which he lives.

Thirdly, language provides the individual with a tool for the exploration and analysis of his own conceptual processes. As we have seen, it is a two-edged tool; it helps us to order our thoughts coherently, but it also imposes upon us the thinking habits of our community, now and in the past, which have crystallised in the grammar and lexicon of the language. Fourthly, language is a means of communication; it gives us some kind of access to the experience of others, the nature of this access depending upon the adequacy of the other person's own linguistic response to their experience and the adequacy of our response to theirs. By observing the linguistic behaviour of others we can explore and analyse their total behaviour and begin to understand their desires and fears.

We saw at the beginning of this chapter that man had survived as a species because of his inherited capacity for social organisation, of which language is the chief instrument, and because of his individual capacity for creative thinking. It is apparent that there is a necessary conflict between the individual and society, and that this conflict is reflected in the nature of language itself. A high degree of social organisation requires the subordination of the individual to the social code; but to have an adaptable social organisation that can meet the threat of environmental change and still survive requires that the individual be allowed scope for his inventiveness. But invention—the thinking of new thoughts—is always a threat to the established social order. The intelligent individual tends to be a disruptive force in society; he has to adjust himself to society to a certain extent because he needs its protection —if he fails altogether to adjust, it is likely that society will destroy him in order to prevent him destroying the social organisation. At the same time, his inventiveness must lead him to try to change society to a certain extent, since he will tend to notice environmental threats before these are apparent to society as a whole; and also because the power instinct is basic, part of the individual's survival equipment.

And so, as a matter of biological necessity, a delicate balance must be maintained between the needs of the individual and the needs of the social organisation. Man, as a species, seems to have survived so far because some combination of genetic traits has enabled him to maintain this balance (whether he can do so much longer is a matter of serious debate). Those things will be called *moral* which tend to maintain the balance; those things which threaten to upset it will be called *immoral*; the intelligent individual will obviously tend to have a slightly different view of morality from society at large, and particular acts which are moral for one generation or for one society will appear immoral to another.

As with morality, so also with language. The intelligent individual needs a coding system as comprehensive and as flexible as possible, one which will give him the maximum help in breaking down his perception into concepts, and offer the minimum obstruction to him when he wishes to express new concepts as a result of putting two and two together. But he learns his language in the first instance from society, and in order to communicate his discoveries he must use a language which society can understand. Once again a balance must be struck, between inventiveness and communicability. In the next chapter it will be necessary to explore the functions that language performs for society as a whole, with particular reference to multilingual communities.

II. LANGUAGE IN SOCIETY

It will be obvious from what was said in the previous chapter that a common language is the expression of a community of interests among a group of people. Many of the current misunderstandings about the role of language in society arise from stating this the other way round and from supposing that the possession of a common language will necessarily give rise to an indentity of interests in a community. It is true that a community is unlikely to feel the closest possible sense of identity unless it possesses a common language; on the other hand there will always be in each community a number of individuals who feel a greater sense of identity of interests with their opposite numbers in other speech communities than they do with people who speak their own language. In the expression 'I get on well with so-and-so because he speaks my language' the emphasis is not on language in the literal sense, but in the metaphorical sense of a community of interests, a common stock of cultural responses. Many an expatriate, living in exile, has come to feel gradually that he gets on better with the people among whom he lives than with his compatriates who come to visit him. We are familiar with the statement that the British and Americans are divided by a common language; behind this paradox lies the truth that an idiom superficially the same on both sides of the Atlantic has its roots in each case in cultural patterns in many ways quite dissimilar, so that apparent ease of communication may remain a barrier to real understanding. English people do not feel impelled to study American English as they study French, finding in that language the reflection of a way of life distinct from their own. The possession of a common language does not necessarily suffice to impose a community of interests and cultural cohesion on Austrians and Germans; cultural cohesion within India, despite a great diversity of languages, is probably greater than the cohesion between English-speaking Indians and other parts of the English-speaking world.

We can best begin by examining the various functions of language in society under the following headings:

Government and the Law.
Education: Primary, Secondary and Higher Education.
Religion.
Culture.

Government and the Law

It might be thought self-evident that for effective government and administration of the law the rulers, the judges and the ruled should form one homogeneous linguistic community. From a vantage-point in Western Europe or North America it might appear as if democracy could not possibly work unless these conditions were satisfied; with an elected Government passing laws in a language which the people could understand, so that they could discuss them; with newspapers reporting the discussion, and politicians addressing the people directly in their own language either face to face or through the medium of broadcasting and television; with the judges and lawyers discussing the law in the same language in which the plaintiff and defendant instruct their counsel. But if these are the conditions for democracy to flourish, then it must be admitted that democracy has very rarely had a chance to flourish because these conditions have rarely existed in history and exist in very few parts of the world today. Even in a comparatively small country like Britain the Welsh-speaking Welsh and the Gaelic-speaking Scots, to say nothing of the Lallans-speaking Scots, need bilingual intermediaries between themselves and the Government, and for dealings in the law. True democracy in the sense of a continuing dialogue between the people and their elected representatives in the Government can only really be achieved in small homogeneous tribal societies. Any community which is governed through the medium of a language other than its own feels itself to be to a certain extent disfranchised, and this feeling, even though latent, is always a potential focus for political agitation. Language is like skin colour in that it is an easily-identifiable badge for those who wish to form a gang or fight against another gang; the reasons for the gang warfare lie deeper than either language or colour.

After the Norman Conquest it was not until the middle of the fourteenth century, when the war against France stirred up nationalist feeling and made the Norman ruling classes feel that they were English rather than colonial French, that English replaced French as the language of government and the law in England. The Poles and the Czechs have rarely known the luxury of being governed in their own language until the past century. Outside the American continent, where there has not yet been time enough for language frontiers to diverge very much from political frontiers, the larger the country the less likely it is that government will be carried on in the language of the majority. In India today, the national language under the Constitution is Hindi; the language most used by the central Government is English; the language of the different state Governments is the majority language of the state in most cases; but there are hundreds of different languages and dialects spoken in India (see Chapter IV) and most of the people have little direct contact with the plans and ideas of the central Government or even of their own state governments. Many of the autonomous republics of the Soviet Union have their own languages but Russian is one of the official languages in each. In China, the Peking dialect of Mandarin is the prestige language of government, not always completely understood, even by other Mandarin speakers, three hundred miles west of the city; a great many of the spoken languages of China, although often called dialects, are mutually unintelligible. The Chinese are fortunate in one way however in that their written language is basically ideographic rather than phonemic. That is, the characters represent the concepts which are represented in the spoken language by morphemes, without reference to the sounds of the morphemes in any particular spoken variety of Chinese; written Chinese can therefore be understood by scholars all over China, in the same way that the numeral signs we use are understood in most parts of the world regardless of what the words are for the numerals in any particular language.

Most of the former colonial territories of Africa have adopted either English or French as their official language, having had indeed very little option because of the linguistic diversity of their territories and the difficulty of imposing any one of the many indigenous languages upon the whole of the population. In East Africa, however, Swahili was sufficiently general for it to become the national language of Tanganyika. In Indonesia, the official language is *Bahasa Indonesia*, a lingua franca based on Malay; but each island of the Indonesian archipelago has its own languages—Javanese, Sundanese, Balinese, Iban, Dusun and many others. The government of the Philippines is effectively carried on in English; as is the government of Malaysia. In neither of these countries, however, is English the native language of more than a very small proportion of the population.

Without multiplying examples any further it will be seen that very large numbers of people in the world today are having laws and other social arrangements made for them in languages which they do not easily understand. Under such circumstances the bilingual who is familiar with one of the local languages and also the language of government becomes a necessary and invaluable go-between. He may be a lawyer, or a civil servant, or a professional contact-man; in any case, his power is greatly increased by the linguistic situation. Any young man who wants to get on in the world will have to learn the language of government if he does not already speak it. Having learned it, he feels that he has joined an educated *élite*, and his command of that language is his badge of middle-class status. He will be reluctant to live any longer where he is probably most useful, among his own people, interpreting the Government's plans to them and helping them to implement them; he will want a white-collar job in the capital and an office from which he need not budge except to go home. He will expect people to come to see him, and will feel that putting something down on paper is equivalent to seeing that a plan is put into effect. It is often claimed that the existence of a large middle-class is essential for the proper working of democracy in our time, but in the multilingual societies with which we are most concerned in this book it often seems as if lawyers, civil servants and contact-men are more parasitic than they are in monolingual societies, just as in England, as long as Anglo-Norman was the language of the law, lawyers were more parasitic than they are today.

Wherever the language of the government and the law differs from that of the mass of the people, plans for economic, agricultural and industrial development are more difficult to make—because the basic research is hindered by the language-barrier—and more difficult to put into effect. Linguistic diversity therefore acts as a brake on economic progress.

Education

Compulsory universal primary education in the vernacular is not exactly new; in England, King Alfred devised such a programme more than a thousand years ago, at the same time stipulating that the international language, Latin, should be taught in the secondary or 'grammar' schools from which the King's Schools of modern England are descended. But in most countries until the present century formal education has been the perquisite of a tiny minority of the total population. In many countries education has always been very closely associated with religion, and has had as its primary aim the production of generations of priests able to interpret and to teach the holy scriptures. The production of civil servants has often started as a by-product of priestly education, but has usually in time become even in such situations the main function of the educational system. In English, the two words *clerk* and *cleric* were originally the same word.

Under such conditions the language of religion has tended to be the language of education and it has not mattered a great deal if this was different from the language of the population at large, since the literate classes were only intended to be a tiny *élite* in any case. Thus for many centuries Sanskrit was the language of education in Northern India, Latin the language of education in Western Europe, Arabic the language of education in the Muslim world (as it very largely still is today). The possession of a common language by scholars facilitated diplomatic intercourse over large areas of linguistic diversity. In each case there has been a body of scripture to be studied by scholars, the very existence of which has tended to conserve a classical form of the language during a period when any spoken varieties of it were diverging more and more from the original in which the scriptures were written down. In Western Europe the medieval church preserved the Latin of the Vulgate for centuries and scholars used it as a spoken language; with the coming of humanism in the sixteenth century scholars tried to reinstate the classical Latin of the Latin authors to whom they looked for instruction and in so doing they hastened the abandonment of Latin as a spoken medium. The language of the Koran is the official language of Islam all over the world, and memorising the Koran is still a major ingredient of Muslim education; but today in Egypt and other Muslim countries the authorities are having to grapple with the problem of providing textbooks for modern education in the modern colloquial Arabic of each region. In China the study by scholars of written texts whose usage reflects that once based upon the spoken language of northern China has preserved a single classical written form of this language in the face of increasing divergence of various spoken forms.

As the language of education in its conservative form based on written texts becomes more and more different from the everyday colloquial usage of the people, however, the content of education itself becomes more and more of a mystery which can only be mastered by longer and longer years of intense study by a tiny *élite*—as happened in China, in Islam, and in medieval Europe—or else there comes a demand for reform and for education in the vernacular. If education in the vernacular is to involve literacy, written forms must be developed which are reasonably close to colloquial usage. The orthography must often be changed, the vocabulary brought up to date.

Whereas in the past literate (as opposed to oral) education was virtually synonymous with learning the international or classical language of the scholars in order to be a priest or a civil servant—that is, it was vocational training—today we have to take into account a new concept of education. This gives pride of place to the development of an integrated and well-adjusted personality, combined with the opportunities for developing the innate potential of each person in the manner that suits him best, and condemns any attempt to make all individuals conform to a common pattern. It is only since mass education became the rule that the conformist pressure of the older type of educational system became a problem. In the days when an academic education was for a small *élite*, by and large only those who were suited to an academic education stayed on at school and went on to the university. The other needs of society were met in different ways—the warrior class were trained in horsemanship and fighting, the boy from a humble home who was good with his hands but not with his brain would be apprenticed to learn a craft. Neither needed to be able to read and write. It is arguable whether universal literacy is in itself a good aim, but at any rate we must accept the fact that it is a basic premise of the way in which modern society is organised. Moreover, the demand for literate education comes from those classes which see themselves at an economic disadvantage without it. This is especially true of the peoples of the newly emergent countries of Africa and Asia. They do not see education as a means of developing an integrated personality, but as the only way to get ahead in the economic race, as of course do many people in all countries.

It will be apparent from what was said in the first chapter about language as a response to environment that the language one learns as a child is the most important key to the formative years of one's development. From this truism many educationists today—perhaps most—go on to argue that a child's primary education at least must be in its native language. *The Use of Vernacular Languages in Education*, published by UNESCO in 1953, states (page 11) that: 'It is axiomatic that the best medium for teaching a child is his mother tongue. Psychologically, it is the system of meaningful signs that in his mind works automatically for expression and understanding. Sociologically, it is a means of identification among the members of the community to which he belongs. Educationally, he learns more quickly through it than through an unfamiliar linguistic medium.'

The writer then goes on to acknowledge and discuss the difficulties of implementing such a policy. It is worthwhile, however, re-examining even the axiom.

In the first place, the expression 'mother tongue' often has very little meaning in a multilingual society. A survey carried out among students in Malaya revealed that hardly any of them came from monolingual homes; the details are given in chapter IV, but here we may note that most of the Chinese students could speak two, and many of them three, languages before they even set out for school. Many of the students found it difficult to say which was their mother tongue. Thus the dogma about teaching a child first in its 'mother tongue' may appear unchallengeable if one is in a fairly simple bilingual situation such as exists in Wales, but is far less meaningful in those multilingual situations with which we are mainly concerned.

Secondly, the claim that 'he learns more quickly through it than through an unfamiliar linguistic medium' is not necessarily true—not very much controlled experimental evidence exists for multilingual societies—and in practice is frequently meaningless because there is so little teaching material available in so many vernaculars. Moreover, apart from innate intelligence the most important factor in determining how quickly a child learns is the attitude of all concerned—parents, teacher and child—towards the medium of instruction and the subject-matter. Until adolescence children find it very easy to acquire new languages provided that nothing happens to arouse their hostility. Children who are used to switching from one language to another in their homes find little difficulty in switching to yet another for school when the education which that language represents is strongly desired for them by their parents. Before he goes to school for the first time at the age of five or six the child is usually prepared by being taught a few words or phrases in the new medium by his parents—to say 'Good morning' to the teacher and so on. If he has older brothers and sisters already at school he will want to join their circle when they discuss school matters in the school language. None of the students in Malaya with whom I have discussed the point has admitted experiencing any psychological disturbance on beginning school at an early age in English; many have said, however, that some of their problems in speaking English correctly could have been surmounted more easily if their teachers had had sufficient linguistic training to be able to pinpoint the difficulty for them.

In most of the newly emergent countries education has to fulfil two urgent tasks which are not always easily reconciled with the ideals of the educationists when the medium of instruction has to be decided upon. The first of these, which I shall discuss again in a wider context later, is to establish cultural homogeneity and a common sense of identity among the members of diverse races and cultures who find themselves members of one state as a result of a series of historical accidents. In some parts of the world—for example, in India—the experiment has been tried of drawing state boundaries so as to coincide as far as possible with linguistic and cultural boundaries; but the danger is that thereby one encourages separatism, and in any case in many parts of the world language-groups are too scattered to make the experiment possible. In the United States the schools have been used as an instrument of establishing cultural homogeneity with great success. Intensive propaganda in the primary schools and the use everywhere of English as the medium of instruction has turned the second- and third-generation children of immigrant Hungarians, Poles, English, Irish, Scotch, Italians, Greeks, Syrians, Puerto Ricans and Japanese into people who think of themselves first and foremost as Americans. In most cases the immigrants came to the United States because they saw it as the land of opportunity for themselves and for their children and because they believed to some extent at any rate in the ideals of liberty, fraternity and equality upon which the United States was founded. It is often painful for them to see their children and grandchildren losing all sense of identity with the immigrant group, and very often reacting strongly against the cultural claims of that group; nevertheless, they have a powerful incentive to accept the process as on balance desirable. In Australia, which is at present subsidising immigration from European countries on a large scale, an intensive programme of English-language instruction and acculturation has been put into effect with marked success. Most of the newly emergent countries would like to instil a similar sense of identity through the schools; they are however not infrequently faced with the problem that the feelings of separatism among the various groups within their borders are stronger than the incentive to unite.

The second function which education must fulfil is an economic one. Nearly all these countries are faced with the problem of how to provide a living for a rapidly increasing population. Agricultural and economic expansion, the diversification of activities, the industrialisation of what have hitherto been plantation or peasant communities, the creation of a technologically-minded and trained middle class, are all urgent tasks. It is necessary that the clever children of the community should learn as much as possible about the sciences that can help to transform their country in as short a time as possible; and the language of these sciences is usually one of the major international languages, with English well in the lead as a vehicle. On the other hand, the local situation in agriculture or economics is rarely exactly that with which these sciences have been dealing in the past. Comparatively few science teachers manage to teach—or even themselves understand—the basic principles of their science; what they usually teach is a body of dogma, a methodology and a technology, and if this is done in the medium of an international rather than a local language the danger is increased that what is learned cannot profitably be applied to the local scene.

There can be no doubt that to educate a child in a language which is not that of either of his parents tends to alienate him from his parents; to educate him in a language which is not one of the indigenous languages of the country tends to alienate him from the culture of his country. If he grows up with one language for the school-room and another for the world outside the school-room he may well develop a kind of dual personality, one side of which—that which is being developed by the ideas which he encounters and the training he receives in school—is sealed off in a kind of linguistic polythene bag from the side which makes the everyday social and cultural and moral decisions. In such a situation very often the child who would respond creatively to his own situation does not do so well at school as the clever parrot. Education through the medium of a foreign language may encourage a kind of opportunism which is not prepared to give any unselfish service back to the community. Teachers in all the English-medium universities and colleges which have been started or developed in the newly independent parts of the British Commonwealth have had to contend with this problem, and from it the main force of the argument for education in the vernacular derives.

On the other hand, the provision of education in the vernacular rather than in an international language often arouses fierce resentment among the students themselves and among their parents. Because of the difficulties in the way of providing higher education and professional training in the vernacular, and the lack of economic opportunities through the vernacular, ambitious students find themselves in a dead end when they finish their primary schooling. The best they can hope for frequently is to become a schoolmaster in a vernacular school. In such a situation the ambitious are frustrated and not infrequently turn to political chauvinism and extreme nationalism, demanding that everybody shall be as handicapped as they are by making the vernacular the sole language for education at all levels. Since the village schoolmaster is often a man of considerable local political influence, a clamour may be set up and political promises made which are then found impossible to fulfil. To implement a programme of higher education and professional training in a vernacular language usually requires an enormous programme of translating textbooks and training teachers. The translation of an advanced textbook in physics must be done by someone who is bilingual in the international language and in the vernacular, and is also a competent physicist. Very few such people exist, and where they do exist their services are urgently required for other jobs. Moreover, a modern textbook of advanced physics can become out-of-date in five years, so that the job has to be done all over again. There is today a world-wide shortage of teachers, and for higher education and professional training many of the newly emergent countries still have to rely to a considerable extent on expatriate help. The expatriates rarely stay for long enough to become sufficiently proficient in the native language to use it as a medium for teaching at an advanced level. A high proportion of those who graduate from the local colleges and universities, who are themselves bilingual and who could be of great use as teachers in the vernacular, have no desire to teach and easily find more remunerative work. In particular, they do not wish to teach in vernacular schools.

The Philippines provides a good illustration of some of the complexities that may beset teaching in the vernacular. Among the 27 million inhabitants of the Republic many Malayo-Polynesian languages are spoken, as well as various Chinese dialects; there is a national lingua franca, Tagalog. Spanish was the language of education and the prestige language when the islands were a Spanish colony and has ever since retained much of its prestige; English has been the medium of instruction in the schools since the first decade of the present century. The Republic recovered its independence from the United States after the end of the Second World War, and recently the medium of instruction in the first two grades of the primary schools was changed from English to the pupil's mother tongue. 'This change was adopted after previous experimentation in many school divisions throughout the country spearheaded by Dr. Jose V. Aguilar's famous experiment on the use of Hiligaynon as the vehicle of instruction when he was the Superintendent of Schools for Iloilo.'[1] But, says Professor Maximo Ramos, the attitude of people in other countries who have great pride in their native tongues contrasts

[1]Maximo Ramos, *Language Policy in Certain Newly Independent States*. Philippine Center for Language Study, Pasay City, 1961.

sharply with 'the freakish attitude of too many Filipinos toward their own native languages'.

> Filipino shoppers in downtown Manila who speak Pilipino to the clerk get little attention or receive haughty stares. One gets prompt service when he speaks English, and prompt, polite service when he speaks Spanish. Some Filipino parents object to their children being taught their mother tongue on the ground that they have learned the language at home . . . . Tagalog . . . made millions of enemies overnight in 1940 by being imposed on the pupils all over the country without warning.[2]

If the population of a country is linguistically diverse, but those diverse elements are mixed up together instead of being in separate areas, it may not be possible to provide school-classes in each area for each different linguistic group. The minorities will always suffer. Even where it is possible to set up separate schools for them the supply of good teachers tends to be more limited than for the larger communities; and so the quality of education tends to be better in some schools than in others, in some languages than in others, and ambitious parents of any race will try to get their children into the school that provides the best education.

It will be seen that no easy solution can be found to the problem of which language to choose for education in a multilingual society. The basic difficulty arises from that conflict which I described in the first chapter, inherent in the nature of men, between the needs of the creative individual and the demands imposed by the social organisation. It is difficult enough in a monolingual society to devise an educational system which can satisfy both. Education is the most important investment any individual or any country makes for the future, and good teachers are more important than any other aspect of the system. The teacher who has a lively and independent mind, who has had a sound basic education and good training, will make use of whatever

[2] Maximo Ramos, op. cit.

material comes to hand, and of whatever medium of instruction seems best in his particular situation. But this ideal is very rarely achieved, largely because the teaching profession is so miserably underpaid in most countries, and so fails to attract the best students. Until this situation is rectified education in the vernacular will fail to produce the benefits for the individual and for society of which it is capable.

Religion

The religious movements which have spread across the world from time to time have been responsible for some major linguistic changes in the countries affected. Once established, they have also tended to provide centres of social and linguistic conservatism. Sometimes the language issue becomes part of a conflict basically religious. The conflict may be between different religious groups, or between an older generation clinging to its religion and a younger generation which is no longer interested. Sometimes, as so vividly illustrated by the 1963 *coup d'état* in South Vietnam, the conflict is between a ruling class which has adopted both the language and the religion of the former colonial power and the followers of an indigenous religious creed.

Both Hinduism and Buddhism have been responsible for the dissemination eastwards from India through South-east Asia, China and Japan of a great many loan-words of Indian origin, but not for the widespread dissemination of any of the Indian languages (except for ritual or court uses). Where these have spread it has been because of emigration. Christianity on the other hand has tended to bring education by mission schools through the medium of a Western European language in its wake—Spanish, Portuguese, French, Dutch and English being the chief vehicles. A great many of today's political leaders in Africa and Asia owe to missionary schooling their fluency in English or French or Dutch, and their consequent ability to get further education overseas and then to play a role upon the international as well as the local scene. The English-medium universities founded by the British in the West Indies, Africa, South and South-east Asia and Hong Kong are mainly secular institutions, but in some cases, as for example in Sierra Leone, they have taken over and absorbed an older Christian mission foundation, and their establishment in most places was only possible because the Christian denominations had already established English-medium secondary schools. The process of secularisation has in a number of countries been extended to a certain extent to the mission schools themselves, which have been integrated into the Government school system as grant-aided schools, inspected by the Ministry or Department of Education and subject to Ministry control over their appointments and curriculum.

Thus in the former British colonies there is still a certain degree of identification between English-medium education and the Christian religion, but the process of secularisation mentioned has, in some countries at least, averted complete identification of the two, and has allowed the continuance of English-medium education even where opposition existed to the spread of Christian missionary activity after independence. Nevertheless it remains true today that the widespread adoption of an international language such as English or French as the national language of a newly emergent country is easier in those countries where no strongly-entrenched system of religious belief exists to challenge Christianity.

In Ceylon the population is, broadly speaking, three-quarters Sinhalese—mostly Buddhists—and one-quarter Tamil, mostly Hindus. About half of the Tamils are descendants of those who arrived from South India as a plantation labour force under the British colonial régime. During the British colonial period the Christian mission schools and the University of Ceylon produced a highly-trained English-speaking *élite*, both Christian and non-Christian but containing a higher proportion of Tamils and of Christians than in the population at large, many of whom entered the public services not only of Ceylon itself but also of Malaya. With the coming of independence the Buddhist monks sought to regain their ancient political influence, and in doing so strengthened the unwillingness of the Sinhalese generally to treat the Tamils as equal citizens. Although under the original constitution Sinhala and Tamil were both official languages, Sinhala was now made the sole official language, and as a result serious racial troubles began. Eventually in 1957 Tamil was given equal status with Sinhala in the schools, and the two languages are gradually replacing English in the university, although English remains in use as an auxiliary language. The Christian mission schools have had a struggle to survive. The English-speaking professional classes have gradually been squeezed out. Ceylon has thus incidentally provided a reservoir of English-speaking professional men, no longer satisfied with conditions in the island, on which other developing countries have drawn to their advantage.

Among the overseas Chinese in South-east Asia traditional Chinese beliefs—a mixture of Confucianism, Taoism and ancestor-worship—are sustained as long as the children go to Chinese-medium schools, but are rapidly eroded when the children go to Christian mission schools teaching in French or English. Thus the desire of the older generation—particularly of the women—to maintain the traditional beliefs has provided much of the momentum for Chinese-medium education.

In Israel, Judaism and Jewish nationalism have been the inspiration of the movement which created the State and brought to it a polyglot Jewish population from all parts of the world. Hebrew is the national language, and the instrument through which the schools have had to create a national consciousness. The teachers have faced a formidable task, and have achieved remarkable results. But the younger generation think of themselves first as Israelis rather than Jews; they are full of national pride, but show little sympathy for or understanding of the traditions of a chosen people suffering in dispersal while awaiting the

Messianic age. In particular they find themselves out of sympathy with the Yiddish-speaking older generation from Central and Eastern Europe.

It should be mentioned here that Christian missionaries have been pioneers in the study of the vernacular languages of most of the countries with which we are dealing. The problem of translating the Bible into hundreds of hitherto unrecorded languages has been a major stimulus in the development of modern linguistics, and many of the outstanding teachers of this subject, particularly in the United States, France, Belgium, Holland and England, are themselves missionaries. Their task is to bring the Christian gospel to as wide an audience and as quickly as possible. Among them we find many of the most active proponents of education through the medium of the vernacular languages. And so, somewhat paradoxically, just at a time when many of the new nations of Africa are trying to extend to the whole population education in English or French on the foundation of a corps of teachers trained by the mission schools, the missionaries themselves are laying the foundations which might in future years make possible the large-scale extension of education in the vernacular.

As a linguistic influence the chief religion to rival Christianity is Islam. Classical Arabic, the language of the Koran, is the holy language of Islam, used in the prayers and scriptural readings of the Mosque throughout the Muslim world from Indonesia to West Africa. Translation of the Koran into the vernacular was until recent years frowned upon by conservative Muslims. In the Arabic-speaking world this presents little problem, although modern colloquial Arabic dialects are of course a long way removed from the classical language. In other countries however there tends to be very little understanding of the Muslim liturgy among the population at large (just as in many Roman Catholic countries there is very little understanding of the Latin liturgy) except where Muslim schools exist teaching in Arabic, as they do in Malaya. These schools in Malaya take their pupils on to the Muslim College where they are trained to become teachers of religious subjects in the state schools or teachers in the Arabic-medium schools, and the best pupils become the Kathis or religious leaders of the Muslim community. Although only a very small proportion of the total school population attend such schools, they form an important element in the religious conservatism of the country and help to preserve the cultural and religious unity of the Malays.

In Africa the Sahara desert roughly divides the Arabic-speaking Muslim north from the Christian or pagan Negro countries to the south. Through trade, however, and through the migration southwards of pastoral nomadic tribes the influence of Islam has been spread around the coasts of West Africa as far as the Gambia, south of the Sahara into northern Nigeria, and around the east African coast as far south as Zanzibar and Dar es Salaam. Ethiopia is in an exceptional position. It has an ancient tradition of Christianity and of close links with the Semitic countries to the northeast; its mountainous inaccessibility in the past kept it relatively immune from the expansion of Islam, and only a small minority of its population is Arabic-speaking. At the recent conference of African states in Addis Ababa the Emperor thought of his country as forming a bridge between the Muslim north and the Christian and pagan south; he has however introduced English in preference to Arabic as the language of advanced education. In the former French territories of North Africa such as Tunisia, Morocco and Algeria, although the *élite* have for many years been trained in French and retain strong cultural ties with France, the vast majority of the population are firmly linked by language and religion with the Arabic-speaking world. Among the Negro countries to the south there is one group—the former French and Belgian colonies—in which French is still used as the official language of education and of the law, and in which close links still exist through

Roman Catholic missionary activity between the French language and Christian education; the Catholic University of Lovanium, just outside Leopoldville in the former Belgian Congo, is a sister university of the Catholic University of Louvain in Belgium. The other group of Negro states comprises the former British colonies, in which, with the exception of Tanganyika, for the time being at least English is the language of education and of government. Some of the newly-emergent countries unfortunately do not fall so conveniently into any of these categories. In Nigeria the official language is English but Northern Nigeria has strong links with the Muslim world. In the Sudan the north of the country, which provides nearly all the administrators and the educated classes, is predominantly Muslim and Arabic-speaking; English is being replaced by Arabic as the official language but the dominance of the northerners is actively resented by some of the southern peoples, whose most vocal and active leaders have received an English-medium education from Christian missions. Arabic being itself an international language, one cannot claim in such a case that the choice of an international language rather than one of the local languages would avert interracial trouble; but the present rather unhappy situation in the southern Sudan highlights the fact that where a language is very closely linked with a religious creed the acceptance of that language by non-believers as a medium of instruction in their schools is made much more difficult.

Culture

It is impossible to enter here into the controversy as to what is meant by culture. Anthropologists use the term to refer to all the traditional customs and ways of life of a community; I am concerned primarily with the arts, and particularly with literature. Nevertheless, a glance at the problems raised by the cultural diversity of a number of the newly-independent countries, using the word culture in its wider sense, may be appropriate before we go on to consider the particular problems of the creative artist.

It is the common experience of the expatriate Englishman who has lived in the tropics for a number of years, upon returning to England, that on the one hand he has a sense of relief as he slips comfortably back into his native culture and finds that he is easily understood, while on the other hand as time goes by he finds England increasingly dull because of its lack of cultural diversity and he starts to yearn to go abroad again. At the same time the English who have stayed at home strike him as parochial and insular, and alarmed because they feel that their way of life is being threatened by the influx of immigrants from tropical countries. He will discover that his fellow countrymen are rarely interested in his travellers' tales of distant parts of the world, and are apt to be unable to distinguish between Indians and Negroes. When the West Indians win a Test Match series Pakistanis share in their reflected glory. 'Chinese food' has become fashionable but he finds it is an Anglicised travesty of the Chinese food he has come to appreciate in the East. The English are perhaps conducting a public examination into the deficiencies of their institutions, but do so for the most part by comparing and contrasting them with those of the United States, another part of the Anglo-Saxon world, or—more rarely—with those of Western Europe and Russia. The stay-at-home feels that the country is full of foreigners; the returning expatriate is sometimes exasperated by the fact that it is too full of Englishmen. His reactions may lead him to an understanding of both the strength and the weakness of being a member of a culturally homogeneous society in a world which requires increasingly an understanding of the strength and weakness of cultural diversification. The educated Southern Englishman is a member of a highly-privileged 'Mandarin' society. His home language is also the prestige language of the country, and one of the prestige languages of the world; it has a remarkable literature, also world-famous. Culturally therefore he is self-confident and assured; so is the educated Parisian; so, once, were the Chinese Mandarin and the citizen of Athens. Cultural homogeneity is a rare phenomenon, however, and so is the degree of assurance which goes with it. Moreover that assurance carries with it always the danger of insensitivity and arrogance towards 'foreigners'.

Most of the countries which we are concerned with in this survey are countries of considerable cultural diversity. Sometimes the reasons for this lie in the pre-colonial past, as in India. Sometimes they are directly due to the colonial period itself; the *pax Britannica* in many parts of the tropical world encouraged alien communities to come and settle and work and trade in secure conditions which they could not find elsewhere; at the same time the plantation economies of many of the former colonies resulted in the large-scale transportation of slave or indentured labour to those colonies from Africa, from India and from China. The political legacy of this situation and its linguistic implications will be discussed more fully in the next chapters; but here ir may be noted that in order to survive as independent states the different racial groups making up each community must learn to live peacefully side by side and become tolerant of each other's way of life. At the same time creative artists are urged to give expression to national as opposed to communal identity. It is no accident that dancing and the plastic arts, and in particular painting and sculpture, flourish more readily in these countries than literature. The painter finds it far easier to evolve an idiom which will reflect the influence of many cultures than does the writer, who has to choose one language out of many. The philosophical works of Rabindranath Tagore may seem rather flat in their English translation, and we are told that they can only be properly appreciated in the original Bengali, a language which few people other than Bengalis speak. On the other hand the English writing of Amos Tutuola, which seems exciting and exotically 'African' to the English reader, seems to many Africans to be simply 'uneducated English', full of interference from Tutuola's native Yoruba. Every West Indian novelist and poet has had to grapple with the problem of whether to address himself to a West Indian audience or to the international audience of the English-speaking world. The vernacular of the West Indian territories is either Creole French or Creole English; the language of educated West Indians in the former British West Indies is English—but with a strong local idiom and accent. The West Indian writer's instinctive response to his environment can often only be given adequate expression through one or another of these media, but people in the West Indies do not buy many books, and have in the past tended to be rather contemptuous of the local product especially if it was written in the local idiom—acceptable for humorous stories and recitations but for nothing else. The West Indian playwright Barry Reckord, when his first play was put on at the Royal Court Theatre in London, had to anglicise some of his most effective scenes, which had been written originally in the Jamaican dialect of Creole English and acted in that medium in Jamaica. His command at that time of standard English for dialogue in his plays was far more stilted and inhibited than his command of the dialect. The West Indian poet Derek Walcott from the Creole French-speaking island of St. Lucia wrote his first poems in a mood of fierce rebellion against the colonial régime and everything it stood for in a style formed by his reading of T. S. Eliot, Ezra Pound and W. H. Auden; in his later poems and plays he has been struggling to give expression to what he feels to be distinctively West Indian characteristics, and has evolved a style of his own in which his native Creole French has played a part.

Thus the creative writer in many parts of the world is faced with a double choice, each choice setting up a tension between his needs as an individual and the needs of the society in which he lives. The first choice is whether to use an international language and so attempt to reach a wide audience and achieve widespread fame as a writer, or to use one of the local languages and be content with a possibly very small audience. Secondly, if he uses one of the local languages, his own—in which he is most freely creative—may not be the 'national language' and he will be subject to patriotic pressure to use the national language instead, in which he may be far less at ease then he is in the international language. He sometimes feels he has no choice but to emigrate. The alternative is often a frustrating cultural exile in his own country.

In considering this aspect of the language problem one must however make a distinction between the French-educated and the English-educated countries. The distinction is perhaps best illustrated by the difference between Creole French and Creole English. Some linguists would deny the status of a Creole language to Creole English, since there exists a virtual continuum from the broad dialect at one end of the scale to standard West Indian English at the other end of the scale, whereas in the former French islands there is a clear distinction and a gulf between the Creole language and the standard French of the island. The objection to the status of Creole English is not I think a valid one since it is equivalent to objecting to a distinction between Spanish and Portuguese as separate languages simply because the dialects of one shade imperceptibly into the dialects of the other. But whereas all linguists and even many educationists recognise the existence of a large number of different educated varieties of English all equally viable for teaching purposes—British English, American English, Australian English, West Indian English and so on—the French insist that there is only one educated variety of French, only one kind of French which should be taught in schools wherever French is the medium of instruction, and that is the educated French of Paris. At the 1962 Brazzaville Symposium most of the French-speaking delegates were unable to agree to a proposal made by the British and American delegates that a research programme should be instituted into the regional varieties of French and English which might be emerging in Africa. They insisted that no such regional varieties existed. It is only fair to add that the Ghanaian and Nigerian delegates also were troubled by the proposal since they insisted that they did not want to be fobbed off with a regional variety of English in their schools. It was for a long time a matter of pride for school-teachers in the United States as in the West Indies to refuse to recognise the existence of acceptable local varieties of English; they insisted that they must teach and their pupils must learn to speak 'correct English'. The insistence on 'correct French', in Africa and elsewhere, has undoubtedly resulted in a standard of French being achieved in the former French colonies higher than the standard of English in many former British colonies, but it has also widened the gulf between the educated and the rest.

The importance of educated regional varieties of English is referred to again under the next heading, 'Contact-Languages'. Creative writing in English in those countries to which English has been transplanted has in each case tended to pass through three phases: imitation, revolt and absorption. In the imitation phase the writer wrote in the European idiom; the young poet modelled himself on Wordsworth and translated his visual experience into Wordsworthian imagery; the novelist would analyse society after the manner of Dickens or Trollope or Marie Corelli—for some odd reason a favourite writer among readers of English in the tropics; he would fail to explore the real tensions of his own society because he had no acceptably literary vocabulary with which to pin them down.

In the revolt stage, which usually accompanied the growth of national as opposed to colonial consciousness, the new generation of young writers rebelled against the artificiality of their predecessors and associated it with subservience; they knew what they disliked, but still had not the literary independence that comes with cultural maturity. The same themes of rejection occur over and over again, but the framework for the analysis remains essentially an imported one—the things they picked upon to find substitutes for were picked upon because they were important in English society, not in their own.

It does not necessarily follow that political independence brings with it the third phase of absorption. So many conditions need to be satisfied before a writer can find an adequate response in English to a society that is not an English society. Nevertheless English has already been stretched and adapted in so many ways that it is a remarkably adaptable language. As soon as an acceptable and recognisable educated variety of the local English idiom begins to emerge the local writer may be encouraged to use it, and so be able to strike a balance between being incomprehensible to an overseas audience and losing touch with his local environment. Some West Indian, African and Indian writers have already achieved this; although the history of English-medium education in Malaya is comparatively short, a distinctive Malayan English is already emerging, speakers of which from the three major communities—Malay, Chinese and Tamil—have a number of linguistic features in common.

Contact-Languages and Lingua Francas

The educated, but distinctively regional, varieties of English form a linguistic bridge between the metropolitan language at one end of the scale and Creole or pidgin-English at the other. No such bridge, it is said, exists between metropolitan French and Creole French. Pidgins and Creoles themselves, however, have played an important part in the past as trade-languages or contact-languages; some contact-languages have developed to the point where they are important vernaculars—indeed, French itself may be regarded as a 'Creolised' Latin—while others are still developing. Some, being trade-languages, serve as a lingua franca between many different linguistic communities.

Linguists generally distinguish at least two phases in the development of a contact-language. In the first phase, speakers of one language acquire—frequently under some economic duress—the rudiments of another language: its basic vocabulary. They tend to pronounce these words according to the phonemic and morphemic patterns of their own language. For example, some Chinese dialects do not contain the set of phonemic contrasts between voiced and voiceless sibilants, fricatives and affricates that occurs in English so that the distinctions between *sip* and *zip*, *few* and *view*, *chill* and *Jill* will be neither heard nor reproduced. Chinese, Malays and Negroes encounter in English consonant-clusters like /sk/, /sp/ and /st/ that never occur in their own languages, and so they break them down, either by chopping off the /s/ or by inserting a vowel: /kin/ for *skin*, /setem/ for *stamp*. Grammatical niceties such as the tense-inflections or the different case-forms of the pronoun in English are not mastered—word-order and context provide the entire grammar, or else grammatical constructions are carried over from the vernacular into the pidgin language. The language-learners go on speaking their own language at home; the 'pidgin' is for contact purposes only, and when using it they will tend to translate literally the idioms and metaphors of their own language, in which they think.

The second stage of development occurs when the 'pidgin' becomes so widely used that it is a more valuable instrument than the mother-tongues; parents then use it to their children, the children grow up speaking 'pidgin' as their first language, their children learn it from the cradle, and develop it into a fully-adequate set of responses to their environment. At this stage linguists call the new language a Creole.

This term was originally used only of the French Creole languages of the West Indies. The process of creolisation has now been recognised as taking place in many parts of the world, not only through the contact of a European language with a local language, but also through the contact of two local languages. Among the European-based Creoles are: Creole French, Creole English, West African

Krio, Cameroons Pidgin, Papiamento of Curaçao, Sranan Tongo of Surinam, New Guinea Pidgin, Creole Portuguese of Malacca, Macao and elsewhere; Spanish contact-vernaculars in the Philippines.

In Africa, the following contact-languages have been described (by William J. Samarin) as the most important of the dynamic lingua-francas: Swahili, Lingala, Bangala, Kikongo, Creole English and Sango.

In the past, pidgins and Creoles have been despised by educated people and ignored by linguists. Today some of them at least are being studied, and are being used for literary purposes; many linguists argue that they are capable of fulfilling a vital educational role in newly-independent multilingual societies. In Brazzaville in 1962 Samarin pressed the case for Sango as a lingua franca for the Central African Republic:

Sango is a creolised language . . . . But being derived from an African language, it is adapted in lexicon primarily to the rural life characteristic of the country and lends itself to use when modern industrial, scientific or religious vocabulary and thought are involved by borrowing from a language that already has a vocabulary embracing these subjects, such as French . . . . The Central African Republic is one of the few countries on the continent of Africa which is so fortunate as to have a lingua franca, the use of which coincides with its national boundaries . . . . Sango could be used to unify the people, as a weapon in fact against the monster of racism . . . . Sango could be used as a means of raising the productivity of the country and thereby the standard of living. Not only can people be efficiently instructed in improved agricultural methods in Sango, but new arts and crafts can also be taught . . . . Sango could be used to teach the rudiments of education . . . . This system would have the merit of training a large proportion of the population which might otherwise never get any education at all, but which if educated could immediately be reached through the government's various media of communication. Sango could serve to raise a citizen's self-respect, for as long as one is illiterate, he feels inferior to his fellow-countrymen. Inordinate pride in one's village or race could yield to pride in accomplishment. Women too would be liberated from the chains of ignorance and instructed in such things as hygiene and gardening.

Can it be controverted that the great threat to the equilibrium of many of Africa's independent states is the dissatisfaction, unrest and antiauthoritarianism that is evident in so many areas? These psychological states and emotions feed on social exclusion, the feeling of being deprived of the good things in life . . . . *Sango has already been used for the benefit of the country.* The earlier administration depended on it for the unofficial interpretation and promulgation of its decrees and programmes. Every court had its interpreter, every doctor his Sango-speaking assistant, every business firm its Sango-speaking foreman . . . .

Samarin did not suggest that Sango should replace French, but that the two were complementary, to unify the country on the one hand and to provide its links with the outside world on the other. If such a programme were implemented it is likely that French would become the model language for Sango, which would gradually change so as to resemble French more closely.

In Sierra Leone, Krio is already well established as a lingua franca with a literature, and could well become the medium of universal primary education side by side with English, which is its model language. In New Guinea, a country of hundreds of languages spoken by small, isolated communities, pidgin Engish or 'Neo-Melanesian' is just entering its 'creole' phase. An enterprising newspaper, *Nu Gini Toktok*, is published in Port Moresby; this, the efforts of the Bible translators, and of linguistic scholars, all help to give the language the status it needs as a genuine lingua franca.

The great advantages of Creole languages are these: first, that they are genuinely indigenous responses to a changing multiracial environment; secondly, that just because of the circumstances under which they have developed they concentrate on the grammatical essentials, and are thus easy to acquire. The situations in which they exist side by side with a model language to which they are closely related, however, possess one quite serious disadvantage: contrary to what is commonly believed by many linguists, 'interference' between the two closely-related language systems can make it much more difficult for the creole-speaking school-child to acquire a 'correct' knowledge of the model language in its metropolitan form, since he finds it difficult to keep the two systems distinct. (Spanish-speakers in British Honduras, for example, tend to speak better English than Creole-speakers.) What is likely to emerge is a distinctive educated local variety of the model language. This, many English and American linguists believe, should be tolerated and even encouraged; the idea is, however, anathema to most French educators, and is also often resisted by the local people themselves, whose pride it offends.

A number of African languages serve as trade languages over wide areas of the continent, e.g. Hausa, centred on Northern Nigeria, Swahili in East Africa. A lingua franca spread by trade is inevitably modified by contact, even if it is not creolised. The advantages of such languages must be taken into account when the question of a national language is considered. Swahili was used by both the German and British colonial régimes for administration and primary education in Tanganyika, and the present Government wishes to extend its use so that it may become the first language as well as the national language of the whole country, with English as the second language.

The private worlds of multilingual societies

There is one aspect of the cultural scene in multilingual societies which is often overlooked. This is the importance to each racial community of having a private world into which it can retreat and discuss the political situation without being overheard by the other communities. If each community has its own newspapers discussion and comment can be carried on in their columns without necessarily inciting anger among the other communities. But the situation may on the other hand excite suspicion. A Government drawn predominantly from one language community may feel uncertain of the loyalties of the other communities and feel compelled to introduce repressive censorship. In Malaysia, which after a long struggle against Communist terrorists has achieved a stable government, the Chinese-medium schools and books imported from China fall under suspicion; the books are frequently banned for no very apparent reason. In Sarawak, where this problem is at present particularly acute, and in Singapore, the Chinese-medium middle schools and Singapore's Chinese-medium Nanyang University are under constant watchful supervision.

III. THE COLONIAL HANGOVER

THE colonial history of a newly-independent country inevitably plays a certain part in determining the linguistic policy of the government after independence. One has to consider under this heading such factors as: the length of the period of colonial rule, and whether during that period there was more than one colonial power in possession; the amount of education provided by the colonial rulers, for what classes, to what level, and in what language; the manner of achieving independence, and relations subsequently with the former colonial power and its allies.

First however we must remember that the moment of achieving independence itself requires certain acts which will symbolise the country's new status to the people at large, many of whom in some countries at least may have had very little idea of the issues at stake. Every new country must have a constitution, a national anthem, a flag, must set up embassies in foreign countries and apply for admission to the United Nations. Some have gone in for more expensive symbols, sometimes rather disastrously; the national airline or shipping line, huge public works such as stadiums which show very little economic return; a palace for the president and motor-cars for ministers. Quite apart from other practical considerations, a national language has sometimes been felt to be necessary as one of these symbols.

The insistence on a national language as a symbol will reflect the manner in which independence was achieved. In Indonesia for example the attempt of the Dutch to recolonise the islands after the Japanese had been expelled at the end of the war led to such bitterness that the Indonesian Government has gone to considerable lengths to repatriate all people of Dutch descent to Holland, including a great many Eurasians who had never even visited Europe and had no roots in Holland, and to proscribe the Dutch language. In India the choice of one out of a great many different vernacular languages—Hindi—as the national language, in the teeth of the very obvious difficulties which such a choice would create, was dictated partly by the determination to eradicate all vestiges of British colonial rule and give a new voice to India's pride in its own ancient culture. In some countries independence has come about at the insistence of one racial community in a multiracial society, and on achieving power this racial community has then wanted to entrench its dominance by making its language the national language of the country, as with Afrikaans in South Africa.

The postwar process of decolonisation has now been going on for more than sixteen years and both the colonial powers and the former colonies have had a chance to learn a great deal about the process during that period, so that the most recently independent countries have been able to avoid some of the mistakes which were made earlier. Where national pride is involved it is often difficult to be coolly rational in making decisions. Sometimes the need to sustain enthusiasm and a sense of national purpose is in itself the overriding practical consideration, to avert the break-up of the newly-independent country. But India, faced with the fantastic magnitude of the task of implementing the national language programme in the short space of fifteen years which was originally allowed, has had second thoughts about this programme and has extended indefinitely the time-limit for the use of English as 'the subsidiary official language'. In Burma, after the order given by the present Government that all teaching at the universities should be in Burmese had led to the resignation of a number of the English-medium professors and lecturers, practical considerations such as the shortage of textbooks and teachers have compelled the reintroduction of English-medium teaching for at least the first two years of the university course. A visiting politician from Ceylon has urged Ministry of Education officials in Malaya not to repeat the mistake that his country had made in trying to implement a national language policy too hastily.

Colonial rule in Burma and Malaya was of short duration compared with Indonesia, and as in Indonesia was interrupted by the Japanese occupation. The Japanese defeat of the European forces in these countries destroyed the myth of European superiority for Asians and very greatly accelerated the demand for independence. It weakened the cultural links between South-east Asian countries generally and western Europe, and strengthened their sense of having Asian interests in common. India after independence declared for a policy of political neutralism and cultural nationalism. At the Bandung conference in Java in 1955 President Sukarno of Indonesia tried to create a firm bond between all the newly-independent Afro-Asian countries out of their common links of anti-colonialism, neutralism in the struggle between the Western allies and the Communist world, and their non-European genetic and cultural inheritance. These rather negative common characteristics have, however, not proved sufficiently strong a bond among the Afro-Asian countries in the face of such very positive threats as the expansion of Chinese Communism and the sometimes conflicting national aspirations of the individual countries concerned. The Government of independent Malaya, formed towards the end of a long, bitter and costly civil war against Chinese Communist forces, became firmly aligned with the Western powers and in particular with Great Britain, so that the cultural links between the two countries have been strengthened rather than weakened since independence. Malaysia, the new Federation, was formed largely to circumvent the threat of Communism from within; the feelings of solidarity between the Malays of the Peninsula and those of the Indonesian Archipelago have evaporated in mutual distrust and recrimination. The Malaysian people contrast their own prosperity with the collapse of the Indonesian economy and view with suspicion the activities of the well-organised Communist party in

Indonesia, while the Indonesians accuse Malaysia of being a neo-colonialist British puppet. The Chinese attack on the frontiers of India caused a dramatic change in India's foreign policy, and created a climate of opinion in which the voices of the partisans of the West were more clearly heard. A country that after independence puts itself into political and cultural isolation certainly lessens its need for graduates with a good command of an international language; but a country which continues to receive expatriate help and to send its students abroad for further training under the Colombo Plan or on Fulbright scholarships or Commonwealth Fellowships by doing so automatically increases the status of the international language in the eyes of its citizens and their desire to receive their education in that language. Indonesia has certainly shown its willingness to accept financial and economic aid from every quarter, at the same time demonstrating very vigorously its political and cultural independence; linguistically, however, the Indonesians have been helped by the fact that having demonstrated their independence by proscribing Dutch, they have felt free to introduce a good deal of English language teaching in their schools and universities. The collapse of the Indonesian economy has not been caused by any unwillingness to accept aid but by President Sukarno's concentration on a policy of achieving a Malayo-Indonesian hegemony under his personal leadership and his neglect of rational economic planning. Now that the cession of West Irian (Dutch New Guinea) to Indonesia has resolved his quarrel with the Dutch, and the Malaysians and the British have taken their place as the targets of his hostility, Dr. Sukarno is once again willing to accept Dutch aid and Dutch technicians.

The feeling that foreign aid brings cultural dependence has perhaps had most effect in Burma. Under the present Government the foreign philanthropic foundations such as the Ford Foundation and the Asia Foundation have been expelled from Burma, together with the English-language teachers supplied by the British Council to the Universities of Mandalay and Rangoon, although the British Council itself has been allowed to continue its operations. In India the language policies of the Government after independence, the fact that many expatriate teachers of English left the country and the rapid and large-scale expansion of education at all levels led to a very serious decline in the standards of the English-medium universities in the country, and so a decline in standards of higher education generally, but in more recent years the Government of India has invited such bodies as the British Council and the Ford Foundation to help them with a programme of providing more and better native teachers of English.

In most parts of the former colonial empires before the war education through the medium of an international language only reached a very tiny proportion of the population. In many countries the colonial policy was that Government provision for education should be confined to vernacular-medium primary schools, and that very often was on a limited scale. It was left to the missions to provide primary and secondary education in the European language. In a number of countries however, such as the Indian subcontinent, the Sudan, West Africa and Malaya, there were founded by one means or another schools run very much on the lines of English public schools to which the aristocracy and the ambitious families sent their children for an English-medium education. Generations of students from these colleges have gone on to English universities and have then returned to their own countries, where today a great many of them are senior members of the professions, of the civil service and of the Government itself. The attachment of these former pupils and their families to their schools is strong, in the English public school tradition, and the schools themselves continue to give an English-medium education, very often with a largely expatriate staff, to the sons and grandsons of former pupils and to the children of the newer *élites*, as well as to numbers of scholarship children from poorer homes. The graduates of such schools have generally had an influence on the professional and administrative life of their country out of all proportion to their numbers. They are sometimes the focus of attack by the anti-colonialists who accuse them of being too thoroughly anglicised. In the former French colonies able local children received their entire education in French, completing it at universities in metropolitan France. They returned to their own countries as Frenchmen, culturally assimilated. Today many of them hold the reins of power, and come under attack in the same way as their English-educated counterparts.

In the West Indies the population is predominantly of Negro descent. After three hundred years of colonial rule and education through the medium of a European language, the vernacular is Creole French or Creole English, the language of education and government in most cases either French or English. The 'national language question' hardly arises in the former British colonies; even in Trinidad and British Guiana, where the descendants of recent immigrants from India make up half the population and where interpreters in Hindi-Urdu and Tamil were until recently needed in the courts, there is unlikely to be any demand for any other language than English as the national language. It is conceivable that in some of the French-speaking islands Creole, rather than French or English, might eventually become the main instrument of education. And in one case at least—that of Surinam—there has been a strong move in recent years for the Creole vernacular, Sranan Tongo, to replace Dutch. Surinam was a colony of Britain for a brief period of sixteen years in the seventeenth century, until it was exchanged by the British for New York, and so came under Dutch rule. But during the period of British rule a dialect of Creole English developed there which has remained the chief vernacular of the Negro population. Since the end of the seventeenth century Dutch has been the official language, and the model language for the Creole, which now shows the influence of Dutch in a great many ways. The incentive today for people to learn Dutch is less strong than the incentive to learn English and French, which are more important as international languages; and so in Surinam the position of Sranan Tongo is stronger *vis-à-vis* Dutch than the position of the Creoles in the former British or French colonies.

Bringing a language up-to-date.

Many of the indigenous languages of the former colonial empires, never having been used for higher education or for official purposes, lack the advanced literature and the specialised vocabulary necessary if they are to become fully viable as national languages. They are not unique in this respect. Nearly all languages have at one time or another had to borrow large numbers of words, and to coin large numbers of words, in order to handle new concepts introduced by contact with other societies or by their own discoveries. Nevertheless, if university education and the law in Indonesia under the Dutch, or in India under the British, had been conducted in an indigenous language, that language would today be better equipped with an accepted and naturalised technical vocabulary, with textbooks using that vocabulary, and with a body of legal judgments interpreting indigenous legal phrasing. The lack of such equipment is a serious obstacle to the national language programmes of several countries. Committees can be—and are—established to enlarge the local vocabulary; but without constant use in the law courts and universities the new vocabulary cannot be assimilated. The committees are often without proper linguistic guidance; in the flush of national independence they may, like the French Academy, embark on a policy of linguistic chauvinism based on a misguided concept of 'language purity', only to find, as Samuel Johnson had found by the time he completed his Dictionary, that 'to enchain syllables, and to lash the wind, are equally the undertakings of pride'. Meanwhile the rapid pace of technical and scientific discovery makes their task more and more difficult. Any newly-independent country which seeks to use one of the indigenous languages as a national language must either devote a very considerable proportion of its resources to word-coining and translation on an immense scale, or see its programme become more and more out of step with what is actually happening in its law courts and universities.

IV. TWO CASE-HISTORIES

1. *India*

There can be little question that India's language problems are among the most difficult in the world to solve, and among the most urgent for economic and political reasons. In a country of about 1¼ million square miles, with a population in 1961 of over 437 million—an average density of 384 per square mile—there were according to the 1951 census a total of 845 languages or dialects spoken. The population is increasing rapidly; a Government that does its best to rely on persuasion and education rather than coercion in domestic affairs must somehow transform traditional village ways so as to increase agricultural productivity—and this is only one of its many urgent tasks. How can the plans of the Union Government be translated into effective action at all levels of society and in all parts of the country? How can the people of India play an active part in local, state and Union government without falling under Communist leadership, which is so active, for example, in Kerala?

There are sixteen states in the Union, and eight 'Union territories' such as the Andaman and Nicobar Islands, Delhi and Goa. In the Eighth Schedule to the Constitution fourteen languages were specified as 'the languages of India'. Of these, Sanskrit is included for historical and cultural reasons rather than because of the number of its speakers; the numbers for each of the fourteen in 1951 were as follows:[1]

Indo-European languages of the Indic branch:

Hindi (Hindustani), Urdu and Punjabi	150 million (no separate figures available)
Marathi	27 million

[1] Source: *India: A Reference Manual*. Ministry of Information, Delhi, 1962.

Bengali	25 million
Gujarati	16 million
Oriya	13 million
Assamese	5 million
Kashmiri	5,086 excluding Jammu and Kashmir, where no census was taken; including these two states, the number of speakers would probably total about 1½ million.
Sanskrit	555
Dravidian languages:	
Telugu	33 million
Tamil	27 million
Kannada	14 million
Malayalam	14 million.

A further 47 languages or dialects were listed in 1951 as being spoken by more than 100,000 persons each; 720 Indian languages or dialects were spoken by less than 100,000 persons each; and there were 63 non-Indian languages spoken.

Each state legislature may adopt any one or more of the regional languages in use in that state, or Hindi, as the language to be used for any or all official purposes. For communication between one state and another or between a state and the Union 'the language for the time being authorised for use in the Union shall be used'. The Constitution provides that the official language of the Union shall be Hindi in the Devanagari script; English will, however, continue to be the official language until 1965, at which date Hindi will become the principal official language. By a recent Government decision English will then continue to be the subsidiary official language for as long as may be necessary. Article 348 of the Constitution provides for the use of English in the proceedings of the Supreme Court and the High Court, and in bills, enactments and other laws.

The partition of the sub-continent at independence between India and Pakistan was done primarily on religious grounds, separating the Muslim communities from the Hindus. Many families were of course divided by partition; thirty-five million Muslims remain in India, forming nearly 10 per cent of the population. (Partition was accompanied by great bitterness and hardship and communal bloodshed, and large-scale upheavals of the population.) Hindus form 85 per cent of the population of India today; Christians and Sikhs make up another 4 per cent, Buddhists, Zoroastrians and members of other religions the remaining 1 per cent.

Linguistically, however, northern India and West Pakistan have more in common than northern and southern India. Hindi, Hindustani, Urdu—these are three varieties of what is basically the same language, an Indo-European language of the Indic branch. *Hindustani* originated as a lingua franca between the Muslim conquerors from Persia and Arabia and the northern Hindus; the name is used today to refer to the colloquial vernacular in India, while *Hindi* is used for the more Sanskritised scholarly and literary form. *Urdu* is the national language of Pakistan; as the language of a Muslim community it naturally borrows many words from Persian and Arabic sources in preference to Sanskrit, and it is used in this form by the Muslims who remain in India.

The major linguistic division in India itself is also basically a division of ethnic origin, between the northern Hindus of Aryan stock speaking Indic languages and the southern Hindus of Dravidian stock, speaking Dravidian languages —Telugu, Tamil, Kannada and Malayalam being the chief of these. The strongest resistance to Hindi as the official language of the Union comes from the Dravidian speakers, who argue that their languages and cultures are at least as ancient as those based upon Sanskrit. Tamil in particular has an ancient classical literature to rival that of Sanskrit.

According to the provisional figures of the 1961 census 23.7 per cent of the population was literate, the rate being nearly three times as high among males as among females. Primary education is not yet compulsory in all states but legislation is gradually being enacted to make it so. The emphasis in the primary schools is on creative activities which will help the child to grow up as a useful member of his community, through the medium of the regional language or—wherever possible—the mother-tongue of the child. Where the mother-tongue is different from the regional or state language, the study of the latter is supposed to be introduced not earlier than Class III and not later than the last year of Primary (or Junior Basic) schooling.

In those states in which Hindi is the regional or state language, it is also commonly the medium of instruction in the secondary schools. In other states, it is either a compulsory or an optional subject in the secondary schools; the medium of instruction otherwise being the regional or state language. In certain areas the introduction of Hindi as a compulsory subject has provoked opposition; when as a result the rules have been modified to make it optional, however, large numbers of students are said to choose it.

In most states prior to 1937 English was not only a compulsory subject but also the medium of instruction in the secondary schools, a situation which dates back to a recommendation made by Thomas Babington Macaulay, at that time a member of the Supreme Council of India, in 1835. (His rejection of the Indian languages in favour of English has had far-reaching results for India.) The mother-tongue or regional language or a classical language (*e.g.* Sanskrit) also had to be studied. Subsequent to 1937 the medium of instruction was changed, and today in practically all states it is either the mother-tongue or the regional language. English is however a compulsory subject in nearly all secondary schools; it is allowed to be the medium of instruction in schools where the students admitted are largely those whose mother-tongue is English, or in schools where it has been necessary to make provision for students who have had to migrate from one part of India to another and would not easily acquire a new regional language.

It will be apparent that language learning must play a considerable part in the secondary-school curriculum of most children, particularly if they wish also to study one of the classical literatures of India. The least-favoured children will have a minimum of four languages to cope with: their mother-tongue, the state language, Hindi and English. The most-favoured will have at least two—Hindi and English. It is not surprising that discussion of the language question bulks large in any official report concerned with education.

Thus, Chapter V of the 1953 *Report of the Secondary Education Commission* (Delhi, Fifth Reprint, 1962) opens as follows:

> The Secondary Education Commission was greatly impressed with the amount of interest evinced in all States in the study of language at the school stage. No subject attracted greater attention and we found not infrequently that strong opinions were expressed on the so-called language controversy.

Some of these strong opinions are reflected in the pages of evidence that follow; evidence given by the speakers of minority languages, by the champions of the various state or regional languages, by the champions of Hindi and those of English.

> The importance of learning Hindi has been stressed, since it has been adopted in the Constitution as the official language of the Centre. Hindi . . . is expected to become the *lingua franca* of the country. It is therefore stressed that Hindi should be made a compulsory subject of study in the school course . . . . It is also stated that a common language like Hindi, if known all over the country, would promote national unity and solidarity. Some of our witnesses have not seen eye to eye with the statement that language necessarily promotes unity. They have referred to many other countries where different languages have been recognised as State languages.

A great deal of controversy also exists about the place of English in the scheme of studies. As a result of historical causes, English has come to be the one language that is widely known among the educated classes of the country. It was stressed by some of our witnesses that much of the national unity in political and other spheres of activity has been brought about through the study of English language and literature and modern Western thought by all educated Indians. They also stated that the present position of India in the international sphere is partly due to the command that educated Indians have acquired over English. Many eminent educationists and scientists have, therefore, expressed the opinion that under no circumstances should we sacrifice the many advantages that we have gained by the study of English. They hold that in matters pertaining to education, sentiment should not be the ruling factor and that what was most urgently needed was that our youth acquire knowledge from all sources and contribute their share to its expansion and development . . . . On the other hand, some of our witnesses have pressed the view that it is unnatural and inconsistent with the present position of the country to prescribe a foreign language as a compulsory subject of study.

A Conference of Professors of Hindi in 1953 at New Delhi resolved:

(i) All institutions in the country should be required to make compulsory provisions for instruction in the language;
(ii) Steps should be taken to make Hindi a compulsory subject forthwith in all Hindi areas and such non-Hindi areas as are ready to take this step; and
(iii) Where regional public opinion is not yet prepared for compulsion, Hindi should be made an elective subject, in which a pass will be essential to qualify for promotion to a higher class.

A Conference of Professors of English held in New Delhi at the same time recommended among other things that English should continue to occupy an important place in the curriculum of secondary schools, and that the aim should be the attainment by pupils of a good working knowledge of English at the end of the secondary stage.

The Secondary Education Commission went on to

observe that there was a serious dearth of properly qualified teachers for both Hindi and English. The standards being accepted were lower than they should be. 'We are convinced that if a language is to be learnt, it should be studied so as to use it effectively and with correctness in written or spoken form.' The failure to maintain high standards in language-teaching was producing serious problems for the universities.

In the final paragraph of this chapter of its report the Commission stated:

> In regard to some of the vocational courses taken in the diversified scheme of studies at High school or Higher Secondary stage, it may be necessary that English should be continued . . . . It has been represented that at present neither the regional language nor the federal language can step into the breach and supply the necessary literature in the particular subject of study for the higher stages of learning. Among the reasons stated were: the great paucity of standard books in the languages concerned; at present several of the languages are still in the process of developing a literature suited to the exposition of modern scientific thought. . . . The necessity, therefore, of reading in English or in some foreign language many of the books now produced in higher ranges of learning cannot be disputed; moreover English is at present the medium of instruction in many universities and will be the language used by the Centre and certain States for some years to come. It is felt that until books written in the regional languages replace books now available in a foreign language, it is inevitable that students will need to have a good knowledge of English to study the subjects in the books available in that language.

The Committee on Emotional Integration, whose Report has already been referred to, was set up in May 1961. It arose out of the Conference of Education Ministers held in November 1960, at which one of the subjects discussed was the distressing frequency with which disruptive tendencies were making themselves felt in the country. While expressing its concern at such tendencies which, if unchecked, it said, might threaten the unity of the country, the Conference stressed the importance of the role of education in counteracting such divisive trends and in fostering unity. The Committee, consisting of twelve distinguished Indian leaders in education and politics, begin their report with an historical survey which draws attention to the long continuity of cultural unity in India, which has absorbed and assimilated to itself wave after wave of invasion and conquest. 'All down the ages, there has been an awareness of an India that transcends all differences of province, caste, language and creed.' It was however true to a certain extent that the whole country had not been united under one government until the British came. Not only did the British provide a unified government, they also provided Indians with a sense of solidarity with one another in their common humiliation and frustration and their desire to achieve their freedom. The English language brought them together on a common platform and evoked their inherent feeling of 'Indian-ness'. 'But it is also true that with the achievement of Independence the forces that divided the people, the so-called centrifugal forces, are reasserting themselves, imperceptibly perhaps, but insidiously and persistently.'

Among the divisive forces the Committee list: caste; communalism, e.g. between Muslims and Hindus; regionalism; provincialism; linguism; frustration among young people, and a lack of idealism. These had been the root of outbreaks of violence, communal frenzy and linguistic madness in certain parts of the country. 'But these episodes, tragic as they were, did not prove that the country as a whole was not functioning as an integrated nation. They only emphasised the need for bringing about a greater degree of integration than already existed.'

By *linguism* the Committee appears to refer to that form of regional separatism which seeks to make the issue of the use of a local or regional language in preference to Hindi or a state language its banner and its cloak:

2.23 What has dragged the problem of Indian languages down to the arena of acrimonious debate is the attempt, by certain people, to make language a cloak for their ambitious designs in other fields, notably politics and employment. That language is the expression of a people's culture goes without saying, but when it is made a slogan it begins to give shelter to hypocrisy and exaggeration, as most slogans do. The fear, real or fancied, that if a language does not receive prominence, those speaking it will be denied opportunities of employment and political influence, is hardly ever expressed. It is generally mixed with other matters, some of which are of very minor importance. The riots which broke out in Assam a couple of years ago are a case in point.

2.24 If people from one part of India elect to take up their residence elsewhere, it is in their own interest to identify themselves with their new neighbours. One of the most potent methods of doing so is to learn the local language and try to speak it properly. At the same time, one can understand the desire of linguistic minorities to have opportunities provided for their children to learn in their mother-tongue. The principle of providing such opportunities has already been accepted by the State governments, but its implementation may meet with some difficulty in the initial stages.

The measures recommended by the Committee to help the primary and secondary schools are designed to ensure that in the first five classes of primary school the child is not burdened compulsorily with more than one language. He will study either the mother-tongue or the regional language; if any school wishes to start the study of another language at this stage, however, it is free to do so. In classes V to VIII the child is to be introduced to the two 'link languages', Hindi and English; but in order to reduce the burden once again, it is recommended that in non-Hindi areas pupils should be allowed to learn Hindi either in Roman or in the regional script. Otherwise the Tamil child, for example, not only has to learn three languages but three different scripts. At the high school stage, however, 'keeping in view the Constitutional provision we consider that . . . *Hindi must be taught in the Devanagari script.*'

The Committee noted with approval the desire expressed

in most states to introduce the regional language as the medium of instruction in colleges and universities:

> 7·30 The importance of having Indian languages as media of instruction from the lowest to the highest stage of education is a matter of profound importance for national integration. There is urgent need to remove the gulf that has existed between the masses of the people and the intellectual elite. For centuries Indian intellectuals had to work in some common language, first Sanskrit, then Persian and recently, English. The gulf between them and the masses of the people has, therefore, persisted. Only the adoption of regional languages right up to the university level will help to remove the gulf. We wish to endorse and emphasise what the National Integration Council said at its recent meeting (July 1962): 'India's university men will be unable to make their maximum contribution to the advancement of learning generally and science and technology in particular, unless there is a continuous means of communication in the shape of the regional languages between its masses, its artisans, technicians and its university men. The development of talent in the country will also, in the view of the Council, be retarded unless regional languages are employed as media of instruction at the university stage.

In its following paragraphs the Committee's report, however, deals sympathetically with the practical problems of implementing such a policy without lowering standards. In particular, text-books must be written or translated in advance of the change-over, and special attention must be paid to the teaching of the link-languages—English and Hindi—when the change-over is accomplished. It will not be sufficient for students to have a 'working knowledge' of English; they must be able to read and understand books and journals, and express themselves with facility in that language. Moreover,

> 7·35 Modern knowledge is tremendously dynamic. India cannot hope to keep abreast of, let alone add to, modern knowledge by relying on translations alone. Not infrequently an article is out of date by the time it is translated; we should take care to see that we are not always a step or two behind the technologically and scientifically advanced countries. In order to ensure

this, our intellectual elite must have a sufficient command of English, and we would add, where possible, of other foreign languages like Russian, German, French and Spanish.

A further reason adduced for having a common medium of instruction in the universities is the need for mobility and intercommunication between different parts of the country to speed the programme of economic development and industrialization. But the Committee was unable to subscribe to the idea that while the sciences required tuition in English the humanities and social sciences did not:

> In fact, we believe, it is the latter, lacking advantages of universal symbols and laboratory work characteristic of the former, that perhaps need tuition in English . . . . The use of English as an associate medium of instruction in the universities is a necessary corollary to the recognition of English as an associate official language and, even more, to the adoption of regional languages as the principal media of instruction.

No apology is necessary for dealing at such length with the case of India, or for quoting at such length from the Report of 1962 Committee on Emotional Integration. This Report is a most important document for any student of the national language question. It is both patriotic (in the best sense of the word) and objective. India has had time since gaining its independence to recover to a large extent from the 'colonial hangover', to experiment, and to assess the results of some of its experiments.

II. *Malaysia.*

When we turn from India to consider the case of Malaysia —a federation which was formed in 1963 out of the states that made up the former Federation of Malaya and the British colonies of Singapore, Sarawak and Sabah (British North Borneo), certain major differences are immediately apparent. Malaysia is a small country of under 10 million people, forced from its inception to fight for its very existence in the face of the active hostility of Indonesia. (This hostility has in fact united the various races of Malaysia as

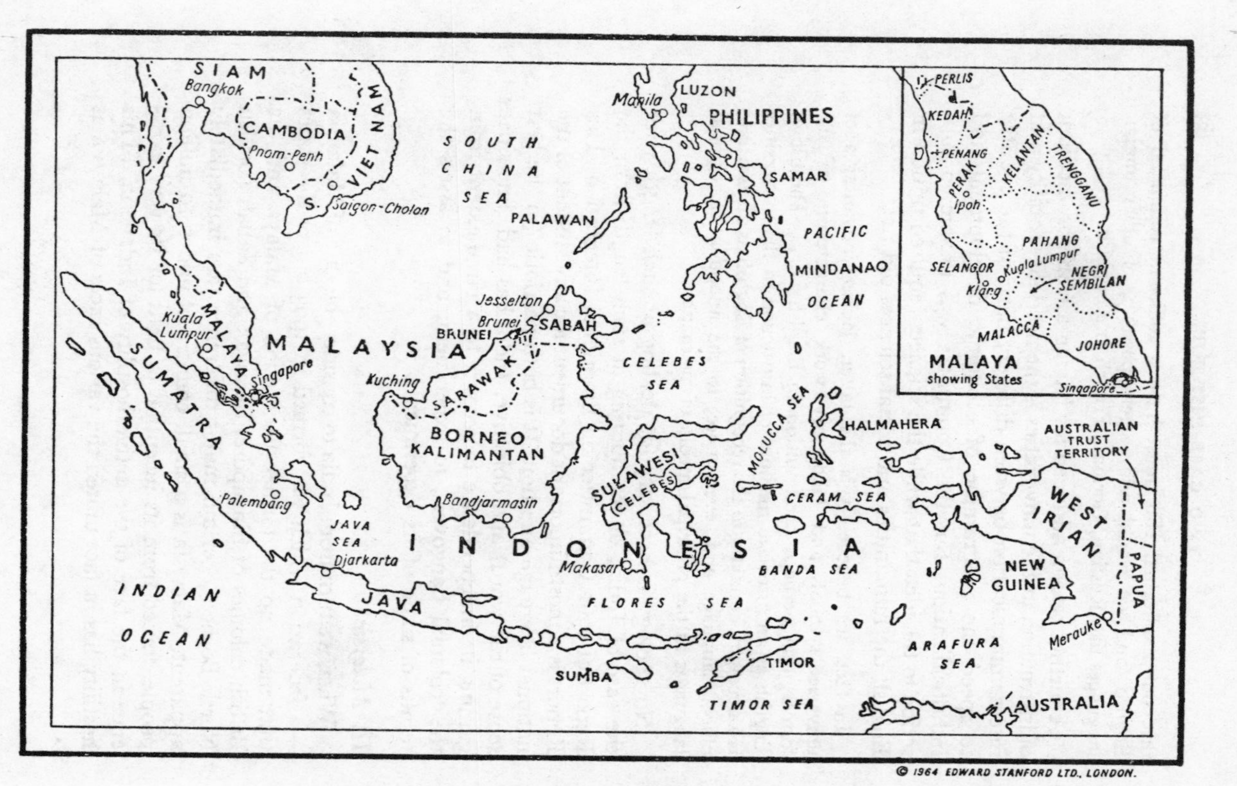

South-east Asia showing political boundaries.

perhaps no other event could have done.) Little more than a century ago the total population of the Malay Peninsula was probably less than 500,000, including the aborigines; Singapore was a fishing village, and the North Borneo territories which are separated from the peninsula by between 350 and 1,000 miles of the South China Sea were very sparsely inhabited. The majority of the inhabitants of Malaysia therefore are either recent immigrants or the descendants of recent immigrants. Each of the three largest groups—the Malays, the Chinese and the Tamils—has its own ancient language, culture and traditions; as have most of the smaller groups. But, in contrast with India, there is no single tradition common to all Malaysians which has any long continuity behind it.

Geographically Malaysia forms part of the Indonesian archipelago, a vast region of thousands of islands covering an area of the globe larger than the United States of America. It is this region which President Sukarno of Indonesia wishes to unify by a close alliance which would include Indonesia, the Philippines and Malaya, or by political domination which would bring the whole of Borneo and the whole of New Guinea under his control. He sees the present division, which gives the North Borneo territories to Malaysia while the rest of that huge island forms part of Indonesia, which also divides New Guinea into the Indonesian territory of West Irian and the Australian trust territory, as simply perpetuating the divisions between the former Dutch and former British colonial empires; while the Philippines, on the other hand, lays claim to Sabah on the basis of the original lease from the Sultan of Sulu by which the Chartered Company of British North Borneo obtained the territory. The claim which is made for the cultural unity of the whole archipelago is based primarily on the ethnic and linguistic affinities of the Malayo-Polynesian language communities, on the traditional role of the Malays as the seafarers of the archipelago, and the consequent use of Malay in one form or another as the lingua franca of the region. The Malayo-Polynesian language community is one of the most extensive in the world, and contains about 120 million speakers. Of these, ninety million are Indonesian citizens.

The Federation of Malaysia has come into being in two stages. In 1957 the Federation of Malaya, which united the nine Malay states and the Straits Settlements of Penang and Malacca under one Government, became a fully-independent member of the British Commonwealth. Singapore however was excluded, and remained a colony. The population of the 1957 Federation according to the census of that year, to the nearest thousand, was as follows:

Malays	2,803,000
Indonesians	281,000
Aborigines	41,000
Chinese	2,334,000
Indians	696,000
Ceylon Tamils	25,000
British	28,000
Thai	21,000
Eurasians	11,000
Pakistanis	11,000
Others	28,000
Total	6,279,000

The above table does not reveal the full extent of the linguistic diversity of the peninsula. The colloquial Malay of the kampongs (villages) shows considerable dialectal variation between the north, the south-east and the west. The language of educated Malays is Standard Peninsular Malay, based on the usage of Johore. Bazaar Malay is the pidginised form of the language, used as the lingua franca of the market-place between different races. There is also an elevated, rhetorical form of the language used in Court circles on formal occasions, known as Raja Malay. Among the Chinese at least twelve Chinese dialects are spoken, many of them mutually unintelligible; Hokkien, Cantonese, Hakka and Tiechiu are the chief, in that order. There is a Chinese lingua franca in each of the main urban areas, which speakers of other Chinese dialects learn, often in a pidgin form: Hokkien in Penang and Klang; Cantonese and Tiechiu in Ipoh; Cantonese in Kuala Lumpur. Eighty per cent of the Indians are Tamil-speaking; Malayalam, Telugu and Punjabi are the main other Indian languages. In Malacca a Creole Portuguese, similar to that of Macao, is spoken among the Portuguese community. Throughout the peninsula, as in Singapore, English is the interracial lingua franca of educated people.

A survey of 200 students in the University of Malaya and in the Malayan Teachers' College in 1962 showed that most of the Chinese students could speak at least four languages with enough fluency to converse in them: they all spoke English, all but two spoke Malay of one sort or another, ninety per cent could speak Hokkien, and eighty-five per cent Cantonese. Those educated in Chinese schools spoke Mandarin in addition, but their English was often only a smattering. All the Malays could speak educated Malay and good English, but only two had a smattering of any other language. All the Indians could speak their own Indian language, English, and Malay of one sort or another; only one claimed to have any knowledge of Chinese. All of the languages mentioned show, in their use in Malaya, the results of contact with the other languages, in their pronunciation, their borrowing of loan-words and in grammatical modifications.

The exclusion of Singapore from the 1957 Federation was a short-term political necessity but a long-term economic absurdity. Singapore is the chief outlet for the natural rubber and tin which form the basis of the Malayan economy; and despite its flourishing entrepot trade Singapore itself could not survive if cut off from the hinterland. Nevertheless, the population of Singapore—over 1½ million—is predominantly Chinese, and had it been included in the 1957 Federation the balance of population would have been changed so as to give the Chinese a majority in the new state. Malaya in 1957 was still fighting a civil war against Chinese Communist guerillas, whose aim was to make the country a Communist Republic. The loyalty to Malaya of the 'Straits Chinese'—those whose families had been settled in the peninsula for several generations, many of them speaking Malay as their first language—was not in question, but that of more recent immigrants from what had now become Communist China was, and a high proportion of those were in Singapore.

Under the 1957 Constitution the Malays of the Federation were given special rights. The Yang di-Pertuan Agong (Head of State) was empowered to safeguard their special position and to ensure the reservation for them of 'such proportion as he may deem reasonable' of positions in the public service, of scholarships and training facilities, and of licences to operate certain trades and businesses. Under this article the rule has been laid down, among others, that four-fifths of all Malayan recruits to the Malayan Civil Service must, for the time being, be Malays. Islam was declared to be the religion of the Federation, although 'other religions may be practised in peace and harmony'. Malay was declared to be the national language, but for a period of at least ten years (i.e. until 1967) English could be used for all official purposes, and was to be used in the Supreme Court and all subordinate courts except when it was necessary that evidence should be taken in another language. Similarly, until 1967 'and thereafter until Parliament otherwise provides', the authoritative text of all Federal legislation was to be the English-language text.

The education policy of the Federation was to establish a national system of education acceptable to the people as a whole which would satisfy their needs and promote their cultural, social, economic and political development as a nation, with the intention of making the Malay language the national language of the country, whilst preserving and sustaining the growth of the language and culture of peoples other than Malays living in the country. It has been laid down that, as far as possible, the wishes of parents must be complied with in the education of their children. At the primary level, parents have the choice of vernacular schools—teaching in either Malay, Chinese (Mandarin) or Tamil—or the English-medium schools. (There are also the specifically Muslim schools teaching in Arabic, but these form a separate small category.) At the secondary level the choice in the past has been between English-medium and Chinese-medium schools. This situation has now changed; within the State education system the choice at secondary level is now between Malay and English.

Malay must be taught as a subject in all assisted schools. The entrance examination to the secondary schools is conducted in the language of instruction which has been used in the primary schools. Within the secondary schools the official examinations are conducted in either Malay or English, and those pupils who have received their primary instruction in some other language enter a Remove Form at the bottom of the school to bring them up to the required standards in the medium of instruction of the school. Thus, Chinese and Tamil children can still be taught in Mandarin or in Tamil in the primary schools, but they are then at an obvious disadvantage if they gain admission to a secondary school. Some of the formerly-assisted Chinese secondary schools which taught in Mandarin have now turned over to being English-medium schools in order to continue to get State assistance; others have become fully-independent and continue to teach in Mandarin.

The University of Malaya, in Kuala Lumpur, is to become a bilingual university as soon as possible. The medium of instruction in nearly all departments is at present English. It is intended however that eventually students who wish to should be enabled to complete their entire education in the Malay medium. Departments of Malay

Studies, Indian Studies and Chinese Studies have been established, admitting students from all racial groups.

The policy of the former Federation Government was thus to unify the cultural and national aspirations of Malaya through the medium of the Malay language, but Government spokesmen have repeatedly emphasised that this policy would not be implemented so as to destroy the cultural life of the Chinese and Indian communities. These reassurances have been made necessary by the realities of the political situation. The Alliance Government of Tengku Abdul Rahman has drawn its support from three parties: the United Malay National Organisation, the Malayan Chinese Association and the Malayan Indian Congress. Its voting strength is very largely Malay but it is supported by many Chinese businessmen and others who see it as the best guarantee of peace and stability for the country. On the right wing there is the Pan-Malayan Islamic Party, which is strongest in the north-east states of Kelantan and Trengganu and stands for conservative Malay-Islamic culture and political organisation. On the left wing there is the Socialist Front, which is predominantly Chinese. The Alliance, in the centre, has seen as its main task that of creating a feeling of national unity in a country of many races and, in the recent past, a number of separate states; it has at all costs had to prevent a split in the country on racial lines. The Malays resent Chinese economic domination, and are determined to entrench their own political domination. The political leaders of the Alliance—most of them Malays—know that they must make the Malays feel more secure if the Alliance is to work. On the other hand, legislation prompted by extremist Malay nationalism, while it would appeal to the right wing, would undoubtedly help to drive many young Chinese and Indians into the opposition camp.

Singapore meanwhile had been granted internal self-government and the People's Action Party had come to power. The PAP is a socialist party and its leader, Mr. Lee Kuan Yew, was formerly regarded as a dangerous revolutionary. Once in power however he adopted a conciliatory attitude and set out to woo the Malayan government since it was obvious that a *rapprochement* between Singapore and Malaya based on mutual trust offered the only hope of independence and economic viability for Singapore. The extreme left wing of his party as a consequence broke away and formed the Barisan Sosialis. The PAP government in Singapore set out to persuade the Singapore Chinese to learn Malay and provided instructors in Malay, some of them from Indonesia. At that time many Malay intellectuals in the Federation looked to Indonesia for cultural leadership, and were more confident of the success of the national language policy in Malaya as a result of the successful use of Bahasa Indonesia—a Malay lingua franca—as the national language of Indonesia. There were however very few Malay-medium schools in Singapore; the majority of the population continued to attend Chinese-medium schools, and a separate university—Nanyang University—had been established and granted a charter in order to provide university education in the Chinese medium. Alternatively, the Chinese went to English-medium schools and to the English-medium University of Singapore.

In 1962 the Malayan Government announced that it was prepared to reunite with Singapore provided that the North Borneo territories of Sarawak, Brunei and British North Borneo could at the same time become part of the new Federation of Malaysia. The Malayan Government desired the inclusion of these territories partly for economic reasons but largely because it was felt that their inclusion would help to restore the population balance between Chinese and non-Chinese in the new State. In the event, when Malaysia came into being in 1963, Brunei, the most predominantly Malay of the North Borneo territories, opted out. The racial composition of Sarawak and Sabah is shown in the following tables:

Sarawak[1]

Chinese	244,435
Sea Dayak (Iban)	241,544
Malay	136,232
Land Dayak	60,890
Melanau	45,976
Others	47,913
Total	776,990

Sabah[2]

Indigenous:	Dusun	145,229
	Murut	22,138
	Bajau	59,710
	Others	79,421
Non-Indigenous:	Chinese	104,542
Immigrant:	Indonesian	24,784
	Filipino	7,473
	Others	11,124
	Total	454,421

Most of the languages of Sarawak, other than Chinese, are closely related to Malay. In Sabah, however, the relationship of the Dusun (now beginning to be called Kadazan) dialects to Malay is not immediately apparent; they seem to be more closely related to the Philippine languages. Numerous Chinese dialects are spoken in each state; in Sarawak, Hakka predominates, in Sabah Cantonese and Hokkien.

The Federation of Malaya was dissolved when the Federation of Malaysia came into being in 1963; Singapore,

[1] Source: 1962 *Annual Report*, Government Printer, Kuching, Sarawak.
[2] Source: 1960 *Census Report*, Government Printer, Kuching, Sarawak.

Sarawak and Sabah having a status within the new Federation similar to that of the Malay states. The new members however insisted on certain additional reservations and constitutional safeguards; as a result among other matters the constitution of Malaysia provides that although Malay shall be the national language of the new Federation, Article 152 of the 1957 constitution should be modified in its application to the Borneo states so as to secure that:

(*a*) for a period of ten years after Malaysia Day and thereafter until the State Legislature otherwise provides, the English language shall be an official language and may be used in the Legislative Assembly and for all other official purposes in the State, whether Federal or State purposes, including correspondence with Federal Ministeries and Departments;

(*b*) for a period of ten years after Malaysia Day and thereafter until the Federal Parliament otherwise provides, the English language may be used by the representatives of the Borneo States in both Houses of the Federal Parliament;

(*c*) for a period of ten years after Malaysia Day and thereafter until both the State Legislatures have otherwise provided, all proceedings in the Supreme Court relating to cases arising in the Borneo States and all proceedings in the High Court of the Borneo States shall be in the English language (subject to the proviso regarding evidence in the existing Clause (4)); and

(*d*) until the State Legislature otherwise provides, all proceedings in subordinate Courts in the State, other than the taking of evidence, shall be in the English language.

As far as the Borneo states are concerned, therefore, the implementation of the national language policy is delayed at least until 1973.

Malay is the most widely-understood lingua franca of both Sarawak and Sabah. For economic reasons, however, English is the most sought-after educational medium, particularly as both states are fairly generously endowed with scholarships for study and training abroad under the Colombo Plan and similar schemes. All the Government schools in Sarawak are now English-medium schools, although in the primary schools teachers still use the vernacular when they need to. In Sabah a start has been made on converting Malay-medium schools to English-medium, and on introducing English into the Chinese schools.

South-east Asia is one of the cockpits of the world. Politically it is the frontier between Communist and anti-Communist; neutralism in this region is a delusion. The British thwarted the establishment of a Communist state in Malaya; the United States is still struggling to repeat this success in South Vietnam, and has poured aid into Indonesia in an effort to bolster the economy and viability of that country. As the result of aid from both Russia and the United States, Indonesia now possesses a large and extremely well-equipped army, navy and air force which Australia, its close southern neighbour, views with considerable alarm. The Communist party is becoming steadily more powerful in Indonesia, and more strongly entrenched in the Government. Malaysia cannot hope to defend itself against all-out attack from Indonesia. Thus the British treaty bases in Malaysia, sandwiched between Chinese Communist expansion from the north and Indonesian expansion from the south, appear vital to the defence of Malaysia itself, to the defence of India and of Australia. Indonesia however would claim that these bases are themselves the cause of her aggression, which is inspired by 'anti-colonialism'.

At the time of writing, Malaysia has just instituted registration for compulsory military service. An Indian member, pledging his support for the measure in Parliament, has commented that all citizens of all races will have an equal responsibility for the defence of the country, and that when the emergency is over they should be given equal rights as well. In other words, he has suggested that the special privileges of the Malays should then be abolished. Malaysia cannot afford communal dissension; it has been and must continue to be an example of interracial tolerance.

It will be seen that a great many economic and political

factors militate against the successful implementation of the national language policy in Malaysia. To these must be added the lack of trained linguistic experts and language teachers, and of bilinguals with an advanced knowledge of their subjects and the time to spare to translate the necessary text-books into Malay. The Language Institute in Kuala Lumpur trains teachers to teach in the Malay medium; the Language and Literature Agency—*Dewan Bahasa dan Pustaka*—has the task of providing the new vocabulary, a national dictionary, and textbooks. But progress has been slow. The Malay-medium secondary schools are still sadly short of both language teachers and textbooks; the teachers very often have to translate English textbooks to the students as they go. Hardly any Malay textbooks exist at the university level for the sciences, and the Faculties of Science, Engineering and Medicine in the University of Malaya feel it is unlikely that they can provide instruction in the Malay medium for at least another ten years, unless they are to accept a disastrous drop in standards and see their graduate students cut off from the universities of the English-speaking world.

Since 1947 the total school population in the various media in Malaya (excluding Singapore and the Borneo territories) has increased as follows:

	1947	1962	Factor of increase
Malay medium	171,000	514,000	3
Chinese medium	189,000	397,000	2.1
English medium	71,000	382,000	5.5
Tamil medium	35,000	67,000	1.9

The Chinese-medium schools reached their peak in 1960, since when numbers have been declining. The rate of increase in the Malay-medium schools is now slightly less than that in the English-medium schools.

Thus although the lingua franca of Malaysia as a whole is still Malay, the chosen medium of education for non-Malays, and for many Malays also, is English. Other considerations aside, the Chinese and Tamils would naturally prefer to be educated in their own languages and preserve their own cultures, but in the tug-of-war between communal and cultural interests on the one hand, and patriotic and economic interests on the other, communal languages are losing ground. The patriotic incentive to use Malay at all levels, however, is not yet strong enough to outweigh the economic incentive to use English. This situation is likely to continue as long as an English-medium education offers better prospects of economic advancement than Malay. Proficiency in Malay is required for promotion in the peninsular Government service but, as we have seen, recruitment into the Malayan Civil Service is in any case heavily restricted for non-Malays by the rule under which four-fifths of the recruits must be Malay. Success in any of the other professions, and even in the Civil Service itself, still requires an English-medium education. Success in business can be achieved through Chinese alone, but even here the pattern is slowly changing.

The Minister of Education has emphasised that both Malay and English are essential to Malaysia, and that both must be taught in the schools. This is a wise statement; if the Malays were to become the only monolingual group in an otherwise multilingual country they would be more severely handicapped in the economic race than they are at present. Taking a dispassionate view of present trends, it seems likely that Malaysia will achieve a greater degree of unity more quickly through the use of English than through Malay, because of the economic attractions of the former language. But if the present Government were to be replaced by one dominated by more extremist Malay opinion, the danger would exist that an attempt to be more ruthless in imposing the national language, without freedom of choice in the schools, would lead to serious inter-racial strife.

V. CONCLUSIONS

One of the working groups of the Symposium on Multilingualism held at Brazzaville in July 1962 listed in their report (not yet published) the factors which affect the choice of a national language, and which ought to be considered by the authorities before they take a decision; they also listed the possible consequences. A free summary of their report, expanded in certain particulars, will provide a convenient framework on which to put together the conclusions that may be drawn from the preceding chapters of this book.

First Factor: The demography and sociology of the language or languages in question. Numbers of native and other speakers, with age, occupation and class distribution. Boundaries of occurrence—geographical, political and social. Evidence of direction and rate of change in status. Distribution and strength of perpetuating mechanisms—e.g. oral and written traditions; educational institutions, mass media using the language; political, religious and other institutions with a vested interest in one language or another.

Second Factor: The past history of the linguistic situation. The nature of past contacts between different language groups, indigenous and foreign. The history of political, social and religious pressure groups. The history of education and literacy in the country.

Third Factor: The structural nature of the languages involved—as described scientifically by linguists; their orthographies; the processes of change to be seen in them, due to dialectal diversification or to contact with other languages. The affinities or lack of affinity between the languages involved, and the ease or difficulty with which each is likely to be learned by the other language-groups.

Fourth Factor: The political, social and economic situation of the country. The extent of the need for foreign aid; the likely sources of that aid. The political, social, juridical, economic and educational situation of various indigenous language groups, and the attitudes towards them of the other language groups. External relations, political, economic and cultural.

Fifth Factor: The organisation and structure of the educational system. Its existing linguistic features. Its resources in finance, teaching materials, teachers and training facilities, both local and available through foreign aid. The control of those resources.

Sixth Factor: The cost of any change in the existing language situation, other than the education costs—e.g. the administrative and commercial costs.

To these must be added the question: how ruthless is the Government prepared to be in implementing a decision that may run counter to the evolutionary linguistic changes taking place in the country?

Each of the above factors is a variable, and in no two countries is the situation exactly similar. No universal solution of the national language question, therefore, exists. The possibilities and consequences, broadly speaking, are:

(i) *To use one or more of the indigenous languages for all purposes.*

Local cultures are thereby preserved; education at the primary level may be easier to provide; children will not be alienated from their parents, nor will one social level be separated from another. But higher education will present serious difficulties, and economic advance is likely to be retarded, unless enormous resources can be devoted to teacher-training and to translation. The country may become isolated, politically and culturally, from the international scene.

If one out of a number of local languages is chosen, national unity may or may not be fostered through it; it is possible that the privileged position given to that language-group will arouse violent hostility from other groups. If several local languages are given equal status, separatism will tend to continue. The adoption of a trade language or lingua franca already spoken at a low level of efficiency by members of all language groups can unify without arousing hostility, and can provide a natural linguistic response to the local environment and the multilingual context (as in Indonesia); but such languages tend to suffer from lack of prestige, which may be difficult to overcome, and from the absence of literary resources which will not develop until the language gains some prestige.

(ii) *To give equal status to one or more local languages and an international language.*

Such a system may provide for a rapid expansion of primary education in the local languages, and of higher education through the international language, thus providing for the economic development of the country and keeping it in touch with the outside world. But the system tends to create an *élite*, uniting the educated of all language-groups but accentuating their separateness as a social class from those with only primary education: the older people, the rural people, the poor. Moreover, if the choice is open to them the more ambitious people will for economic reasons choose education in the international language, and the impetus to improve the local languages and the educational facilities in those languages will be weakened.

(iii) *To adopt an international language for all purposes.*

Education from the lowest grade to the highest for all language-groups in an international language can unify all the younger members of a multilingual society, within a period of fifteen to twenty years, provided that the resources of trained teachers—local or expatriate—are adequate. If they are not, there will be a progressive modification of the international language (with possibly increasing inefficiency of the solution) down the social scale and outward from the centres of instruction. Some degree of modification, of adaptation to the local scene, may in any case be desirable. But this third solution will inevitably divorce the younger generation from the culture of their parents, and may provoke popular resistance, nationalistic or ideological.

Decisions about a national language policy are normally made by politicians, not by linguists; and for political reasons which may seem valid at one moment but may have lost much of their force ten years later. The younger generation who have not had to fight for their independence may not share the cultural and nationalistic ideals of their parents. The mass of the population may have very little choice over education; those who have a choice, or create a choice for themselves, are likely in a newly-emergent nation to be motivated by the desire for economic advance. If the people feel frustrated in this respect, no policy is likely to succeed. An empirical and pragmatic approach to the problem is therefore desirable, and policies should be worked out within the limits of what is feasible.

Given the opportunity, however, the linguist can make his contribution to resolving the problems that may arise from whatever decision has been reached. Any decision is likely to involve bilingualism for many—probably most—of the population. The linguist can carry out the basic research, describe the various languages involved in a given situation, prepare contrastive studies, forecast the difficulties that speakers of one language are likely to have in learning another, and guide the preparation of teaching materials which pay special attention to these difficulties. He can thus help the country to make the most effective use of its teachers, and so reduce the damage to the educational system which might result from a mistaken decision. He can train teachers, not only in language-teaching but also in the sympathetic tolerance that comes with the objective study of multilingual situations. He can advise on the best means of bringing a language up to date, and the most effective mode of translation. Help with linguistic research and training is, and should continue increasingly to be, a most important element of foreign aid to the newly-independent countries.

But perhaps even more effective would be aid to increase the salaries of teachers, in such a way as to induce the best teachers to stay in the classroom. Any educational system which promotes the best teachers to be administrative headmasters, or Education Officers, or Inspectors; any system which offers the schoolmaster so little prestige and salary and such arduous working conditions that he will jump at any opportunity to leave his profession to become a UNESCO 'expert' or a Professor of Education—these are self-defeating. Agencies such as the Peace Corps and Voluntary Service Overseas, which supply working schoolteachers to the newly-independent countries, are doing a more useful job than those which supply 'experts' and advice; but no country can staff its schools with expatriates and no national language programme can hope to succeed until the best local graduates are retained in the teaching profession.

SELECT BIBLIOGRAPHY

Government of India, Ministry of Education. *Report of the Secondary Education Commission* (1953), Fifth Reprint, Delhi, 1962.

Government of India, Ministry of Education. *Report of the Committee on Emotional Integration*, Delhi, 1962.

Government of India, Ministry of Information and Broadcasting. *India—A Reference Manual*, Delhi, 1962.

Paul Henle (ed.), *Language, Thought and Culture.* Ann Arbor: University of Michigan Press, 1958.

Proceedings of the CCTA/CSA Symposium on Multilingualism, Brazzaville, 1962 (not yet published). CCTA/CSA, Watergate House, York Buildings, London W.C.2.

Maximo Ramos, *Language Policy in Certain Newly Independent States.* Philippine Center for Language Study, Pasay City, 1961.

Frank A. Rice (ed.), *Study of the Role of Second Languages in Asia, Africa, and Latin America.* Center for Applied Linguistics, Washington D.C., 1962.

John Spencer (ed.), *Language in Africa—Papers of the Leverhulme Conference on Universities and the Language Problems of Tropical Africa.* Cambridge University Press, 1963.

UNESCO Monographs on Fundamental Education: Vol. VIII, *The Use of Vernacular Languages in Education.* Paris, 1953.